YOU FAILED ME

A JOURNEY FROM NEGLECT AND ABUSE
TO ACHIEVEMENT AND SUCCESS

JOHN LOVE

Two Penny Publishing
850 E. Lime Street #266
Tarpon Springs, Florida 34688

TwoPennyPublishing.com
info@TwoPennyPublishing.com

For permission requests and ordering information, email:
info@TwoPennyPublishing.com

Library of Congress Control Number: 2022908917

Paperback: 978-1-950995-70-7
eBook also available

FIRST EDITION

For information about this author, to book an event appearance
or media interview, please contact the author representative at:
info@ twopennypublishing.com

ENDORSEMENTS

"John's writing immersed me into his childhood and took me on an emotional journey of sadness and hope. This book is a must-read for every teacher, police officer, social worker, neighbor, and friend."

R. Patterson
Law Enforcement

"You can really put yourself in the author's frame of mind in the story. Coming to terms with the pains of the past without forgiveness presents raw feelings many people may have."

G. Compton
Business Owner, Youth Mentor

"As an educator, this book caused me to reflect on my own actions in dealing with children."

L. Stevens
Educator

This journey began as a project of reflection and perhaps healing; as it developed, I became conflicted about its impact on some of those who would read this.

This story, my story, is tragic and painfully true.

This is not a self-help story, nor is it a story filled with happiness and joy. But if this story helps even one person become more aware of a child in distress, then the inner pain I have resurrected in writing this will have been worth it.

***This book is dedicated to my grandmother,
Dorothy Love, 1921 – 1991.***

*The woman, who more than anyone else, gave
everything she had to protect me from the monster
that my mother brought into my young life.*

To my wife, Johanna, *thank you for encouraging
me to complete this project and encouraging me to
be vulnerable and candid about my journey. Thank
you for helping me find the courage to complete this
book and for wrapping your love around me when the
memories came back in the form of pain and sadness.*

TABLE OF CONTENTS

FOREWORD

This is a must-read book for all parents and professionals working with children! *You Failed Me* is an inside look into the world of one person's childhood trauma, abuse, and neglect. The author's unimaginable journey through childhood, and his resiliency to overcome his past—and thrive—is inspirational. As an elementary educator for 30 years, I am reminded of how impactful my interactions can be with those children who may be suffering in silence.

Kim DiCataldo
Career Educator

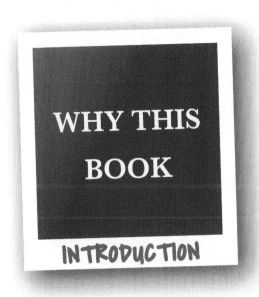

WHY THIS BOOK

INTRODUCTION

I chose to write this book for many reasons—the most important one is my desire to share my early life candidly with my children. I hope this book will help them better understand me and the people who raised me. My life is my life; the journey I have been on for 50 plus years is the journey that has made me who I am today and one that continues to impact me.

From there, perhaps this book can provide an opportunity for others to have a candid look inside the life of a child living in poverty, abuse, and despair. Either way, this is my story. A story that in some ways may seem tragic and, sadly, probably very familiar to other people who grew up poor or in homes lacking love and care.

I hope that this book will land in the hands of one teacher, one police officer, one doctor or nurse, one Social Worker, one neighbor—anyone who might find themselves hearing that little voice in their head telling them that something is not right with a child they know. If this book causes just one person to have a heightened sense of awareness of abuse, neglect, or despair, then I will consider it a worthwhile project.

I bet if you asked 100 people if they care about their neighbors or for the people in their community, 99 out of the 100 would answer with a strong, resounding "YES." Most people believe that. However, if that is true, how is it that we can have such poverty and despair in a country filled with so much wealth and promise? How can a child grow up neglected and abused despite countless adults surrounding them? How do the safety nets put in place to protect the innocent so often fail? Perhaps it is because we all get tunnel vision in our own lives, that we fail to see the lives others live. Maybe it's because we see how others live and don't understand how to help. Perhaps because we are the ones creating such trauma in the lives of others. No matter the reason, it is our reality. It is my opinion that we, as a society, fail the vulnerable every day.

As you think of situations in which, you too, may know of a child in distress, you may wonder how is it that you can help. Help doesn't need to be anything more than a kind word, a caring voice, or simple attention to let the child know you are there and that they are not alone. If you suspect a

YOU FAILED ME

child is being neglected or abused, you should seek advice or input from appropriate agencies. At the back of this book, I have listed resources that you may use to help someone vulnerable or at risk.

THE ADULTS?

CHAPTER 1

To explain the world I grew up in, I feel it's essential to describe the people who brought me into this world as well as those who were part of making me what I have become—for good or bad. To give you a better understanding of these people, I am providing you with a deep dive look into each of them.

Mother: *Yes, Mother. Mom, for me, suggests a person who nurtures or cares for one's offspring. Mother is a being that gives birth—I have a mother. Throughout my entire life, my mother failed to be a mom. She failed me from conception, and roughly five years after she had me, she failed my little brother starting with his birth. What caused my mother to fail so badly at parenting and her choice of men?*

My mother was born in 1945, the oldest of four children. Her childhood home was the typical post-WWII household with two parents who worked in professional careers, one a train engineer and the other a nurse. There was a large extended family in Rochester and nearby towns who all played a role in my mother's life. Church and religion were also key pillars to my mother's upbringing. My grandparents were proud and devout Presbyterians that were actively involved in their church. My mother lived in a modest single-family home in a safe, peaceful city neighborhood filled with diversity in ethnicity and religion. All the children attended public schools and of course, Sunday school each weekend. All four of the children graduated from high school, some started college (although none finished) and each one of them was loved by their parents and were shown proper examples of how to raise a family. The Love household was a typical post-WWII middle-class American home to a "T." I have seen many photographs of what appears to be an ordinary, happy middle—American family. Photos of my grandfather sitting in his recliner while the kids played at his feet. Pictures of my grandmother cooking in the kitchen or doing one of the girls' hair. Pictures of my uncle in his Army class A's and the girls in dresses presumably for dates or special events. So many images depict typical teenagers of the 1950s and 1960s. My grandparents owned their own home, worked hard, provided, and protected. They attended church and lived as good Christians would in those times. I have never heard anyone say a cross word about my grandparents or their parenting. On the contrary, Mr. & Mrs. Love were respected and respectable people.

After graduating high school, my mother enrolled in college but never completed it. I doubt she ever attended a class despite being registered. This is odd because one of my mother's unique characteristics is that she seems very intelligent. While she is not the best communicator, I would bet that she has an IQ higher than the average person. I am surprised to this day at some of the thoughts and opinions that come from my mother's mouth, even as she nestles into her mid-seventies. As a child, I recall that my mother would volunteer as a teacher's aide at my grammar school. Yes, the woman wouldn't get a paying job, but she was somehow willing to take a teacher aide position for free. Helping kids in a classroom came naturally to her, but caring for her own children did not. Her being an aide was either her way of giving back or her way of keeping an eye on me—there would be a good reason for that.

My mother gave birth to me in the spring of 1969. I was not planned, simply put, I was the result of a fling. In the 1960s, peace and free love was all the rage. Because she was unwed, and not in a romantic relationship with my father, her pregnancy was hardly a welcomed event in the Love household. As my grandmother would tell me when I was older, my mom was dating a nice guy in graduate school at RIT (a local college), but then she met someone else and got pregnant. When looking at old photos, my grandmother would say that my mom never took very good care of herself and was always "running around" with men.

After giving birth to me, my mother moved out of her parent's home, with or without me—I do not know. I do know that at some point very early in my life, I lived with my grandparents. I lived with them for most, if not all my first years of life, without my mother, until a point when she married the devil. I was around 5 or 6 then. I do not know what took place in my mother's life between my birth and the age of 5, and I highly doubt that I would get any sort of straight answer if I asked my mother. Regardless of who was raising me, my mother met and began dating the person she would later marry—the man who shaped my childhood world more than any other person. The man that, for me, is the essence of evil. He was from a small town two hours away but nearby to where my great uncles and my mother's cousins lived. Perhaps it was there, in Auburn NY, that she met the devil.

My mother had opportunities in her life growing up that many people, better people, never had. My mother had a loving childhood, great role models as parents, a stable middle-class home, and even a pathway and encouragement for higher education, and yet, she failed herself and others. As an adult, my mother had many opportunities to escape her hell and yet ignored each one of them. Those around her, including me, begged her to escape her hell, to leave the man who abused us all—yet she stayed. For those who do not know of my mother's upbringing, it would be easy to surmise that her life choices and parenting skills, or lack thereof, must surely be a result of her upbringing—how wrong one would be. To this day, I can't understand how my mother, who was raised in a God-fearing, middle-class home, could make such poor life choices.

My biological father: I don't know much about my father's life before he met my mother. I would often wonder what his upbringing was like. I had no point of reference or information that offered insight. I do not know if my father was brought up in a loving home or in a cold one. I don't know a single thing about his childhood or early years.

I never had the chance to call my father, "dad" because my mother, for whatever reason, saw to it that my father was not in my life. I am not sure if I am the result of a relationship gone wrong, a fling, or a one-night stand. Perhaps my father treated my mother in a way that caused her to have no contact with him. Whatever the reason, she seemed to like him enough to have sex, at least once, and that was enough to create me. I remember meeting my father one time as a child. I am guessing I was maybe 5 years old. We met each other at a paternity test, in which I had to have blood drawn, as did my mother and the person who I was told was my father. I remember a tall man with dark hair, well-dressed, sitting in a room with my mother and me and saying nothing to us. When he left the room, my mother said, "That's your dad, and he doesn't want anything to do with you or to pay for you." Was that true? Did he not want me, or was that her choice? Or did he not want her, and by default, me either? No matter the truth, that is the only recollection of my father from my childhood.

Years later, I had a chance to meet my father, it was brief, dismissive, and led nowhere. My wife had reached out to the man my mother claimed was my father—his name is "Joe." He was a high-ranking person in the transit industry. My wife tracked him down, and my father accepted her call and agreed to meet with me for coffee—I was thirty years old. By this time I had an eleven-year-old son of my own, and I was confused about my desire to meet him and what I hoped the outcome would be. I know I wanted a relationship, but more than that, I wanted to know why he wasn't in my life. I also wanted him to know how rough my life had been. The day came for me to meet Joe (my suspected father), and we sat together for about 30 minutes. Joe told me that he knew my mother, and did date her, but so did other men he knew of back then. He said they were not in a real relationship and that he didn't know if he was my Dad. Apparently, the results of the paternity test taken when I was a kid came back inconclusive. Although Joe was cordial, he was also honest in his feelings. Joe made it clear that although he would be willing to retake another paternity test, he had his own family and wasn't interested in a relationship with me. Going into the meeting with Joe, I was prepared to ask so many questions and share so much of what I experienced growing up. I was prepared for anger, sadness, confusion, and more—yet sitting across from this man who looked nothing like me, I said nothing other than "thank you for meeting with me." Given that fact, and considering that I felt no instant connection, we said our goodbyes and parted company. You can't make up

YOU FAILED ME

for time lost or create feelings in an instant despite what you may see in movies.

Many years later, with the advent of home DNA testing for family lineage, I took a home ancestry test. As luck would have it, I had connections, and wouldn't you know it—that guy in the coffee shop twenty years ago, his brother and nephew came up as my uncle and cousin. That guy in the coffee shop that looked nothing like me and whom I felt no connection to 20 years ago was my father after all. I don't regret not sharing my feelings with him then or not asking more questions or even not keeping in touch over the years. At that moment, sitting across from me in the coffee shop, he was a complete stranger. There was no "Hallmark" moment or father/son bonding with a happily ever after ending. Since taking the ancestry test, I have met some of my father's family. To be certain this connection wasn't just a mere coincidence, I took a second home ancestry test from a different company and so did one of my newfound cousins—again a perfect match. There is no doubt that Joe is my father. Through these meetings, I learned a great deal about Joe. It seems Joe was a popular guy when he was younger. A ladies' man. He drove nice cars, was good-looking, had a way with words, and that led to having a way with women. Unfortunately, I also learned that Joe would not be easily contacted. It appears that my father's wife is very controlling and rarely lets him near a phone or to stray from her side. My father, who is now in his eighties, is as out of reach as ever.

The one upside to this connection is that I no longer wonder who my father is.

Shortly after my DNA testing, I was contacted by another DNA match, this time, a half-brother. The person who contacted me was in search of his genetic family. He was put up for adoption at birth and had no connection to his biological family. As it turns out, he was born just a few months after me. Yes, Joe had at least two women pregnant at the same time—and apparently neither had a relationship with him beyond what it took to make babies. My half-brother was raised in a relatively average suburban home. He was and is loved by his adopted parents. He has grown up to be a nice guy and I am glad to have met him. As a child, I had often wished I was put into foster care. How ironic is it that I have a sibling who was put up for adoption. When I consider my upbringing vs. that of my half-brother, I think he was dealt the better hand.

I did have the chance to see Joe one more time just recently. His brother, my uncle whom I never met, passed away. I was invited to the funeral by my new found cousin. When Joe walked in, I saw a frail, hunched-over man who walked with a shuffle. In looking at Joe, it was hard to imagine the frail man standing there, in his Velcro sneakers and cane, was once a ladies' man wooing women into his arms. I looked at Joe from afar, wanting to say hello but afraid it would take away from the sanctity of the calling hours. Instead, I just found a corner and stared. I stared at this man, wondering why he was not in my life. Standing and staring and internally wanting to scream at him; wanting to ask him why. Why weren't you there for me? Why did you let me live as I did? Did you know how bad it was? Did you know about me? Did you ever want to see me? So many questions and this was my chance to say something, but I didn't—I just stared.

As I left the funeral home, I walked past Joe, never stopping. But as I passed by, perhaps for the last time ever seeing him, I said, "How ya doing, Joe?" Never pausing to hear his answer or making eye contact with him. My cousin later told me that Joe asked him who I was, and he told Joe—"that's your son" and Joe said nothing. Yes, I am his son, that man from my childhood who had the chance to engage with me but didn't, and now all these years later, I had that same chance to engage with him, and I did not.

I doubt I will ever see Joe again. I don't think of him as my dad, I think of him as my father. There is no emotion attached to the thought—but the thought sometimes enters my mind. What if? I wonder what life would have been like if he was in my life. The kid in me would say I wish he was, but the adult version of me says I'm glad he wasn't because my journey would not have led me to who I am today if he was. I have accepted that Joe and I will never speak. He is old, frail, and in the last years of his life. There is little we would have to say to each other at this point, anyway, so why bother. I am at peace at least knowing who this person is so I don't have to wonder any more who it was that made me, who is my father?

Harold: aka Lucifer; that is how I often refer to my stepfather. Harold was from a small town a few hours from Rochester. He had at least one brother that I remember, but I don't know of any other siblings. I don't recall much about his family or visiting them. Harold served in Vietnam, and I couldn't tell you if he peeled potatoes or was a war hero—I just know that as a child there was a picture of him in his class A uniform that hung in our living room, and I often wondered how such a professional-looking guy could turn into such a stumbling drunk. I can't imagine him being much more than a grunt soldier if he ever saw action at all. I respect that he served, but I would bet the house that he was drafted and not a volunteer. He was not made to be a defender of freedom and liberty.

My mother met Harold while visiting her cousins a few hours away in Auburn, NY. She would go there often to be with her friends and family. As I understand it, she continued with her freedom after I was born and would spend days at a time in Auburn, running around with friends and cousins doing what people in their twenties were doing in the 1960s and early 1970s. Harold was just back from Vietnam, and somehow, someway, he met my mother. If I were to bet, it would be that they met in a bar—I doubt he was ever sober. Her meeting him, dating him, marrying him, would change the course of my life forever. To this day, I fail to understand what positive value he brought to her life. How does a woman even speak to a bum in a bar? What value do they see in this person? I am not victim-blaming, but is it unreasonable to expect people to have a greater sense of self-worth? Either way, my mother meeting Harold would start a relationship that, over time, brought fear and pain to many people, helpless people, one of them was me.

Harold never held a solid job a day in his life. He was the neighborhood drunk no matter where we lived. Sure, he had the title of "superintendent" in a few apartments, but it meant nothing and paid barely enough for his beer. Rather than working, Harold spent most days lying on the couch with a beer sitting on the floor next to him along with an ashtray filled with spent cigarettes. A day of work for Harold was waking up, walking to the store to buy beer, walking home, drinking, getting drunk, and sleeping. Sometimes, too many times, he would mix it up a bit by beating the shit out of my mother. If it was a special day for him, I would become the target. This was Harold's career—drink, get drunk, abuse someone, and so on. He stunk like filth and looked as if he slept under bridges. I doubt he showered more than once a month, at best, and he was the definition of lazy. I can think of no adjective that adequately describes this excuse for a man other than repulsive. I recall him lying on the couch in filthy jeans and always an old, filthy, button-down shirt, and dirty socks that rolled off his bony legs. His hair was curly and often resembled a rat's nest. Harold had no teeth, so watching him eat was tough. He had a beard that had never seen a trimmer and always had his beer close by. Genny beer was the local beer of choice, it was cheap and readily available at most corner stores.

Grandfather: John W. Love, the person for whom I am named after. My grandfather was much older than my grandmother. He was born in Scotland in 1901 and immigrated to the U.S. in the 1930s, the same way many others in his time did. He arrived penniless and eager to make his mark in America. He eventually settled in Rochester, NY along with his brother and a few cousins. He served in World War II, lost his brother in the war, came back to his adopted land of America, and began a family. My grandfather enjoyed a middle-class life with the help of his wife. They raised four children and contributed to their community. My grandfather lived life as one should, loving his family, his neighbors, and his country. He loved tea and toast, grilled cheese, and tomato soup—made with milk, and only with Ritz crackers. He would play old Scottish songs on a small organ, and would sing these songs to my grandmother and me all the time. My grandfather loved to play the horses and would go to the track every Sunday, as long as he went to church with my grandmother first. I remember my grandmother telling me a story of her only speeding ticket— of them getting pulled over on the way to the horse track. As she would tell it, church ran long, my grandfather was mad that he was going to miss a race, so my grandmother sped and got pulled over. I don't know if they made the first race or not, but she would tell that story many years later every time she saw someone speeding past her. "Are they late for the races?" she would say as cars passed by.

My grandfather died in 1975 when I was just 6 years old. He lived a good life and was gone too soon from mine. Apparently, he got up from bed one night and was found the following day on the bathroom floor. My grandmother, who was 20 years younger than him, was devastated. I lived with them then, and I remember my aunt carrying me to the neighbor's house, telling me my grandfather was dead and that I needed to spend the day with the neighbors while they helped grandma with things. I vividly remember his funeral and I remember going to his grave every Sunday with my grandmother. Fresh flowers for the vase or tending to the ones that were planted. Wreaths on holidays, flags on veteran's day, and tears every time we went. My grandmother loved him, and she was lost without him. She would sit in a folding chair at his grave and cry. She would talk to him about life, about family, and their marriage. My grandfather was a good man. I have just a few memories of him, but the ones I have are vivid and happy.

Grandmother: Grandma; Hero; Angel; Protector; Dorothy Love, born in 1921, a mother to four children, a nurse, a deacon in her church, a God-fearing lady who loved life. She was from a large family. She had four siblings and remained close to them throughout her years. There were plenty of weekend visits to her siblings which I got to tag along.

My grandmother loved to cook—always from scratch. I loved going to the local farms and picking fresh strawberries, cherries, or tomatoes with her. She would wink at me as we picked fresh strawberries or cherries and tasted them right there in the fields. My grandmother was often seen with an apron around her waist and flour on her hands. She baked, cooked, created amazing treats, and always, yes always, made sure her grandchildren had food in their mouths.

My grandmother loved to travel—but only if she drove. She would drive to Florida to see cousins, to Massena, NY, to see the ships pass the locks, or to Letchworth Park to see the changing of the leaves. My grandmother's car was her way of seeing the world, one mile at a time. She loved to explore new roads and would often just hop in the car and go for a drive. She would frequently drive until her tank was half full, then turn around and make her way home. It was her way of seeing new areas. She was outgoing, never afraid to ask for directions, and always willing to take a chance to see something new. I think I learned my love of driving, rather than flying, from my grandmother. To this day, I will find myself thinking of her when I am on new roads, in new areas, or seeing new sights from the windshield of a car. Some of my most enjoyable times driving are when I am alone, and she often enters my mind during these times.

My grandmother was a woman who gave everything she had to her children up until the day she died—penniless. A woman who would not eat so that others could. Her children took complete advantage of her, taking whatever she had rather than earning for themselves. My mother was at the top of that list. My mother borrowed money constantly, never repaying it. My mother, and to some level, at least one of my aunts, were responsible for my grandmother going deep into debt with high-interest personal loans so she could lend the money to them—never to be repaid.

My grandmother, more than any other person in my childhood, was the absolute essence of my protector. On more nights than I can count, she would come to my rescue. She always found a way to eventually save me from the evil that lived in our home, if only for a short while.

My grandmother will be referenced many times in this book. Each time I write of her, I know my throat will become choked and my eyes will fog over as they are now. If nothing else, sharing my story is going to bring me back to many memories of her. There is no possible way I can articulate the depth of my love for her, the longing I have for her, and the hope I have that she can somehow see me today. So much of what I am today is a testament to her everlasting love for me. I miss her and would give anything in the world to have more time with her. My grandmother passed away in 1991, shortly after my son was born. I wish my son could have grown to know her and I wish she could have known him more.

These people, the good and bad, are the people who were the adults in my early life. For me, I was lucky to have some and cursed to have others. Either way, for me, my life began with these adults shaping it. Regardless of the journey, they get the credit.

A CHILD IS BORN

CHAPTER 2

Although I am sure some people can remember their earliest years, for me, I do not. I only know of the first years of my life based on stories shared or from pictures. There are two competing stories of my early years, one from my mother, and one from others such as my grandmother, aunts, and uncle. My mother's version describes a sort of utopian childhood. To hear her talk about me as a small child and the life I had, one would think she was a glowing, loving mother from day one. There is little mention of the fact that I lived with my grandparents full-time. The reality is that my mother's only story of my childhood that has been told over and over as if it was the main subject of her parenting, is one of going to a Niagara Falls amusement park when I was very small. I have seen the few photos and they are the only photos my mother has ever been able to produce of any family outings. One story. One event, that a whole early childhood image is built upon.

I tend to believe the second version told by other family members. Sadly, this is not the brightest version, but it is what I believe to be the truest. If you were to ask my grandmother, she, and others, would describe my early years as being neglected by my mother. Neglected from birth by my mother, cared for instead by her parents and her younger siblings. Stories of my aunt Edna (the youngest of four children) caring for me while my mother was out with her boyfriends. Stories of my grandpa being mad at my mother for having a child out of wedlock, for not taking care of me, for not doing what is right. Yes—right from birth it seems I was destined to have a tough go of it. Well done mother—YOU FAILED ME.

What cannot be denied is that I lived with my grandparents full-time from my first day on earth. I am not sure if it was my mother's choice or my grandparent's insistence, but for whatever reason, my grandparents were tasked with raising me. As I understand it, my mother also lived in their home on and off after my arrival, but the day did come that my mother moved out and I stayed behind. Even when my grandparents sold their home and bought a smaller home in the suburbs, I went with them. I have been told that my mother was not in the picture very often. I clearly remember living with my grandparents, going to church on Sundays, playing outside, climbing trees, and taking short day trips to parks for picnic lunches. I don't recall ever feeling a longing for my mother. She was not in my life, and I was either not aware or did not care that she was not around much. It just didn't matter. My earliest memories of life are memories of my grandparents' home, my home. A place where I was loved and cared for.

When I was old enough for school, being that I lived with my grandparents, they enrolled me in a school near their home. I started kindergarten and made quick friends. I had a relatively normal first year of school—go to school, come home, have lunch, ride my big wheel, play with friends, have dinner, and the next day repeat. Much like most other children, life was normal. I am not sure I ever questioned why I lived with them, I just did, and life couldn't have been better. My life was seemingly ordinary yet looking back—it was amazing.

CHANGE COMES QUICKLY

CHAPTER 3

One day when I was five, it all changed for me. My mother showed up at my grandparents' home—my home—as she did from time to time, but this time with a man by her side. A man she said was now my dad. I don't believe I had ever seen him before, but my grandfather knew of him as I recall and I don't think things went all that well. I remember my grandmother and grandfather talking about this man and my mother's desire to take me away. Within a few weeks of that first visit, my mother was back with this man she said was now her new husband. This time they were there to take me home with them. It all seemed to happen so fast. I didn't know why this was happening. I was playing outside and suddenly, my mother called for me, told me to get in the car, and that I was going home with her. I turned to my grandfather and grandmother, standing on their porch and I ran to them. My mother pulled me away and somehow got me into the back seat of her old car. I remember crying, kicking, and screaming. I was being kidnapped! What was happening and why? What did I do wrong?

Either way, I ended up at home with my mother and this man that I was told to call dad. I don't remember how long I was at my mother's house, but I don't think it was more than a few days. For one reason or another, living with my mother came to an end as quickly as it started. I recall my grandparents appearing one day at my mother's apartment and telling me I was going home with them for a while. When you're a kid, you don't comprehend what is happening, things just seem to happen. Either way, I was back with people who loved me. I was soon back in a home filled with love, safety, food, and comfort. For whatever reason, my mother let me go home with the people that loved me, the ones that I loved. People that were more like parents to me than grandparents.

It was during this time that my grandfather passed away. I was six years old and didn't really understand that he was gone forever or what it meant. My grandmother would tell me that grandfather was taken by God to his forever home in Heaven because God needed more angels. Why did God have to take him? Why then or ever? When you're a kid, it seems that there are more questions than answers. Death is not something children understand, nor do they understand the pain and sorrow in the hearts of the adults around them. For vulnerable children, death can turn their world from

YOU FAILED ME

challenging to catastrophic in the blink of an eye. This is one of those pivotal moments that can occur in a child's life, which can bring chaos and stress to everyone involved. Our society offers few safety nets to help family members navigate the time after a caregiver's passing.

My grandfather's passing didn't just change my grandmother's life, it changed mine too. It began a toxic tug of war for me between my grandmother and my mother. There was a constant feud brewing between the two of them about where I was going to live. My grandmother always told me she would keep me safe—she did her best, but without my grandfather around, Lucifer was too strong…

Over that summer, my grandmother and I had settled into a new normal without my grandfather. My grandmother had little time to grieve the loss of her husband. Not only was she still working full-time as a nurse, but she was also raising me and taking care of her home. She spent time at the cemetery on Sundays and learned to mow the lawn and trim the hedges. Soon after my grandfather's death, my grandmother took early retirement from her job at the community hospital, partly I believe so she could take care of me. When my grandfather was alive, he would watch me (he was retired) while she worked. With my grandfather gone, there was no one to watch me and I believe my grandmother did what she had to do, giving up a career she loved to be able to care for me.

Life seemed to move on, and God and church were still the centers of my grandmother's life. The horse races after

Sunday church that grandpa loved so much had now been replaced with cemetery visits, but otherwise, life seemed to be moving on. It was just the two of us, and together we were doing alright. My grandmother never let me see her pain and always had a loving smile for me.

As summer ended in 1975, there was a battle brewing between my mother and my grandmother. I would witness this firsthand or hear it on the phone. Whenever my mother would show up at my grandmother's, I would head outside to play. Many times, her visits, often with Harold (my new "dad"), often turned into an argument that ended with my mother storming off.

It seemed to be a regular occurrence—one that ended in tears for my grandma each time. I would sometimes hear her sniffling as she stood at the kitchen sink or sat in her room. I don't think there was ever a formal custody arrangement for me to live with my grandparents and I feel as if my mother held the threat of taking me away over my grandmother's head. I doubt she wanted me; I was just a pawn for her to get what she wanted.

Grandma and I traveled a bit the summer my grandpa passed away, maybe just to get away from my mother. We spent time visiting my great uncle and his family of six kids in Auburn. They lived in a big house with a yard filled with Crabapple trees, a swing set, and more. Some of my best memories as a kid were visiting them. They were kind people who we enjoyed spending time with. We would also spend time on the weekends visiting other friends and relatives, or just traveling around the Finger Lakes looking for the perfect spot for lunch. Grandma turned every trip into an adventure.

One night while returning from a trip to Auburn, my grandmother's car was hit head-on by another driver. I was asleep in the back seat when it happened. I have seen the pictures as an adult, and I don't know how either of us survived. The car was twisted in a way that would suggest death as the only outcome for the occupants. We were both okay, the worst thing that came from it was the loss of two small containers that were filled with small cars I carried everywhere. This accident resulted in yet another argument with my mother, her threatening to take me away because, as my mother put it, I could have been killed, as if it was my grandmother's fault. Ultimately I stayed with grandma—at least for a while longer.

One day as summer came to an end, my mother appeared once more. I was playing with a friend nearby when I heard my name called out over and over. It was a voice I recognized as my mothers; she was calling for me to come to her. I said goodbye to my friend and walked up the hill. I had no idea this would be such a turning point in my young life—I was six years old.

As I walked to my grandmother's front yard, I heard my mother yell, "Get in the car, you're coming with us." I ran into the house and into my bedroom and cried. My grandmother came in and told me I had to go with my mother. "John-boy, be good, I will come and see you tomorrow," she said as she sat on my bed next to me. My grandmother was such a gentle person and always so happy, but there was sadness in her eyes at that moment. This woman had lost her husband and now I was going away—she would be alone. I was just a kid but I felt her sadness. I hugged her and we walked outside. *"Get-in-the-damn-car!"* my mother said and I complied. In the passenger seat sat Harold—smoking, not saying a word. We drove away from my home into a world that was anything but loving.

Mother, YOU FAILED ME.

As I sat in the back seat crying, my mother told me that I had to live with her because welfare found out I was living with my grandma. Apparently, this was a problem because they were losing food stamps and benefits if I didn't live with them. She said maybe I could go back to Grandma when things settled down, but I would have to go to school where she lived for now.

> *Harold never had a real job, neither did my mother.*
> *Welfare was their income and my not living with them*
> *was a threat to them having a place to live.*

My mother said I had a new brother and they needed to keep a roof over their head. The next words that came out of my mouth introduced me to a whole new level of pain and fear in an instant.

"I don't want a new baby," I cried. "I hate you, take me back!"

In what seemed like an instant, Harold told her to pull the car over. We were barely away from my grandmother's house. Maybe he was going to throw me out—I could run back. This is great! Wrong thought. Harold jumped out, opened the back door, and began hitting me with his belt. He hit the top of my legs; I moved to the other side of the seat and the next hit caught my back. I tried to open the door, but he pulled me across the seat and told me to shut the fuck up unless I wanted more. I am certain I just sat there silent the rest of the way to their house. This would be my first beating, my first moments of terror—but not my last.

Harold, YOU FAILED ME.

MY NEW HOME

CHAPTER 4

I don't recall the rest of the ride to my mother's house. We arrived at a large building with at least four apartments. It was in a part of our city that then and now is a tough neighborhood. We went inside and up some stairs where my mother told me to go and sit in the living room. There was a couch and a TV—not much more. She told me everything would be okay but that I had to be a good boy. She said that this was my home and Harold was my father now. Looking back, I can only wonder, what the hell was she was thinking? This man just beat the shit out of your kid on the side of the road, he has no job or means to support us, and you chose him? Really? Of course, at six I didn't think that, I just thought, I hurt, I was scared, and I had no one to help me— Mother, again, YOU FAILED ME.

Pretty quickly my grandmother showed up at our apartment, it seemed like it was just a few hours later. She brought my big wheel, a dump truck, a few other toys, and a bag of clothes. I asked if I could go outside and play, and Harold said yes. I remember playing on the slope of the yard, with no grass, just some dirt. I noticed my grandmother's car in the street and went to it. It was unlocked and I got in. Who knows what I was thinking, perhaps I could escape, I don't recall. But I remember feeling safe. I remember spending a few minutes laying on the front seat and just hoping her being at my house meant I would soon be leaving with her again. My grandmother eventually came out with my mother close behind her. They called my name, and I got out of the car. My grandmother kissed me on the forehead, slipped me a few pieces of butterscotch candy, and said she would see me soon. I sat there in the dirt and watched as she drove away—I would see her drive away many more times, every time wishing she would stop, back up, and take me with her. I would watch her drive away just hoping she would come right back for me.

> *Each time grandma drove away I would hide somewhere and cry for her to come back. Cry to God, cry to the sky that she would turn around and take me with her. More than once I would stare at her car driving away and hope that when the brake lights would shine, it meant she was coming back for me.*

YOU FAILED ME

As my grandmother drove away that day, my mother called me into the house. It was time for supper. I am sure it was either fish sticks or boiled hot dogs on bread. That's about all my mother made—oh yeah, maybe chicken. She called it "par-boiled" chicken. I don't know who the hell ever invented that, but imagine a piece of chicken cooked in boiling water—it smells awful and turns a revolting shade of gray/white. Either way, dinner was served. To this day, I won't eat boiled chicken or fish sticks, but truth be told a cheap hot dog on a slice of bread is still kind of appealing.

When bedtime came, there was one bed, I think it was maybe a queen size. I lay on one side, mother and Harold were on the other. There wasn't enough room for everyone so I asked if I could lay on the couch. My mother said yes and I quietly left the room. The couch was old, and I had no blanket or pillow. I was alone in the dark, in this awful place and I am sure that I cried myself to sleep like I would many more times in the years to come. The couch became my new bed for some time after that. This was the same couch Harold would lay on all day. I had to smell him—I could never escape him. He had control of me while awake, and while I slept. The monster never left me alone.

My grandmother came and visited again a few days later. I remember seeing her pull up and I hoped she was there to take me home with her, but that wasn't the case. She was there to drop off some food and spent a few minutes speaking with my mother outside. She never ventured in, I am guessing because Harold was inside. I can only assume that either she was concerned for me or perhaps my mother called saying that we needed food, either way, she brought a few bags of groceries. I am sure she struggled with my mother attempting to raise me and she did her best to be present whenever possible. My grandmother would drop in unannounced from time to time, always with groceries in hand—it was almost like her passport to visit.

As my grandmother left that day, I walked her to the car. She asked me if everything was okay. I told her how Harold hit me really badly. She asked where and I pointed to my legs and my back. She raised my shirt, and I can only assume that she saw bruises because her reaction was instant. My mother was standing at the front door and the two began to argue about what happened to me. With that, Harold came to the front door and told me to get in the house, he also told my grandmother to mind her own fucking business. Yes, I remember—as if it was just now—"mind your own fucking business." That would be the last time I saw my grandmother for a while. She was an old woman who was no threat to Harold or my mother. They held all the cards and there was little she could do.

I did my best to avoid Harold. He scared me. I would stay outside as much as I could. I would only go in when called and then I would try to be no more than a shadow in a room. I played with matchbox cars and would carry myself off into a world of make-believe. Playing with cars allowed me to escape my reality. I could be anywhere, be anyone, doing anything when I played with my cars. There was no Harold, no mother, and no abuse, hunger, fear, or stress. There was always a floor, a chair, or even just my lap to play with cars on no matter where I was. Matchbox cars were this kid's escape from reality. To this day, I still have a collection of them, and I have tried to replace all the models I can remember having as a kid.

TIME TO MOVE

CHAPTER 5

We didn't live in that apartment for very long. One day my mother announced we would be moving to a new apartment, and that I had to help get packed up to move. Moving didn't matter much since I didn't have any friends in that neighborhood anyway. When you're poor, moving, which is often the result of eviction, is quick, sloppy, and unemotional. You get out as fast as you can with whatever you can carry. There is no planning or preparation. To move you need a few things:

1. Lots of black garbage bags—they are strong enough to throw over your shoulder loaded down with clothes and not tear open.

2. It helps to have a car, but at this time, and others, we used "borrowed" shopping carts for most things and

then borrowed a car for the few pieces of furniture we had.

3. You only need a couple of boxes for dishes.
4. Maybe a broom to sweep up—maybe.

That's it. Moving doesn't require wrapping fragile stuff, organizing labeled boxes, or any sort of process. Moving many times as a kid evolved into how I pack for travel today—throw your stuff in a bag and walk out. Today I use a suitcase, but I still find myself throwing stuff together at the last minute.

Leaving the apartment on Garson Ave, we moved to South Fitzhugh St. #141, apt 1. This was our new home. Our apartment was a very small one bedroom that was rundown and roach-infested. So bad was the infestation that at night, before walking across a floor, you would need to turn on the lights so the roaches would scatter; otherwise, you would step on them barefoot. I can tell you what roach poop looks like, what roach eggs look like, and how to tell if roaches have been around. Roaches can and do climb in your bed, fall into your food, and crawl on your skin. When living with roaches, you always check your food before putting it in your mouth, shake your clothes before putting them on, and rinse a glass before using it. The apartment was small, but it was what it was. The building had fourteen apartments and I spent many hours riding my big wheel around the building or playing in the many halls. There were no other kids in the building, it was mainly filled with older people. It stands today not much different than it did back then, and I often drive by to look at it. The memories are not good, but they help me appreciate where I was, and where I am.

The neighborhood was relatively safe. It was made up of mostly poor families, mostly minorities, living in apartment buildings or run-down single-family homes that had been converted to multi-family residences. It was close to downtown Rochester, which at that time was bustling with shopping and office buildings. I was enrolled in a new school, which was just a few blocks away. I would walk to school from our apartment, crossing at least three busy streets, alone at six years old. Apparently, this also meant I was old enough to walk to the corner store from time to time and get items my mother or Harold requested on a note, usually accompanied by food stamps.

As time went on, Harold aka Lucifer, seemed to get more violent. He would sit on the front steps and drink his usual few six-packs of beer each day, then stumble in and lay on the couch. Frequently during his drinking, my mother and Harold would argue. He would hit my mother, beat her until the neighbors pounded on the door or the Police showed up. He would hit my mother with a pillow and kick her in her stomach. I can attest that a pillow in a pillowcase at full swing can do some damage, and yet, leave no marks. He would also beat me, but he was smart about it, always on the bottom or the back, never where the bruises would be seen.

When the police would show up, the story was always the same. My mother would refuse to press charges. There were no domestic violence laws in the early seventies, so Harold had no penalty unless my mother agreed to press charges. The usual routine would be, Harold beating her, she screams for help, neighbors call police, police show up—my mother refuses their help, police walk out. Then round two, Harold apologizes, she threatens to go jump in the Genesee River or commit suicide, Harold cries, she cries, and all is forgiven—until the next time.

Sometimes it was different. If my mother had a bloody lip or black eye (she had plenty), the police would arrest Harold. He would be taken off to jail for the night. If my mother failed to show up in court the next day, he would walk free—mother never showed up for court. That was always the case—always. I am certain my mother made the conscious decision to stay with Harold out of either fear or blind love. There is no other logical reason. My mother had a safety net in her parents, yet she chose not to use it. My mother had other alternatives as well—none of which she used. Instead of leaving the abuse, my mother stayed. In her own way, she inflicted a form of abuse just as bad on me and my little brother by threatening to commit suicide when Harold beat her. I recall begging her, holding her leg, crying for her not to leave and not to jump off the bridge into the river. My mother brought as much mental anguish to my young life as Harold brought in physical pain. My mother chose to live with this monster and take the beatings, that was her choice, but it was also her choice to let him beat me. That decision will never ever be forgiven—Mother, **YOU FAILED ME AGAIN**.

YOU FAILED ME

The police visited our apartment regularly and mostly just went through the motions of dealing with a man that was an abuser, and a woman that wouldn't hold him accountable. Each time the police came, I hoped they would take Harold away. Make him leave forever. I didn't understand how things worked or why he was allowed to keep returning to hurt us more. As a child, I sat in the back of a police car many times while officers did a police report with my mother in the front seat. My mother never wanted to press charges and I often wished they would arrest her too.

The police were my heroes and I looked up to them. One more than the rest, the one that I often saw take Harold away in handcuffs. He always drove car 233. I speak of him in my acknowledgments and am grateful to have crossed his path. On far too many occasions I would find myself sitting in his car while he wrote a report. He would talk to me about how I was doing in school, his job, and very frequently he would say something that, over time, stuck with me—and does to this day… "Just because you live like this, doesn't mean you have to be like them." As a small child, I didn't really understand what that meant, but as I grew, I began to get the meaning of his words. He was telling me in his own way that my future did not have to be defined by the people that were raising me or the environment in which I lived. This officer, more than others, showed compassion and care. He understood the impact his words could have on me.

As time passed, my mother would let me spend most weekends with my grandmother. We would spend most of our time together taking day trips here and there. Our adventures seemed spectacular then, and today, I find myself occasionally trying to retrace our paths. Scottish doings in Rome, NY, a nearby lake for lunch and swimming, or a park for sandwiches and time tossing rocks in the canal. As I look back, I believe that my grandmother took this time with me to help me escape from the world my mother held me hostage in. Back then it was just a day trip, but looking back, it was a rescue, it was a temporary escape, it was God working through her to help me.

I recall a time we traveled to see the cargo ships travel through the locks in Messina, NY; My grandmother had somehow misplaced her billfold along the way, and therefore, had no money or credit cards. Fortunately, she had a small amount of money in her purse for emergencies and determined there was enough for gas to get home and some dinner on the way. We left for home and as we drove it got dark and she grew tired. She pulled into a motel and spoke with the person inside. I guess she got the okay from the people to park in the lot for the night. They gave us blankets and pillows and my grandmother turned it into a campout. The following day, we continued our drive home and she made everything seem as if it was just part of a planned adventure. That was the kind of person she was. She persevered, she provided, and she protected as best she could.

Eventually, we moved from apartment one to apartment two across the hall. This was a big deal for me because it meant I could get my own bedroom. In apartment one, my brother and I shared a room so getting my own bedroom was a very big deal. My bedroom was a place to escape to. Without exaggeration, much of my time spent indoors would be spent in my bedroom. No TV, not much to do, but it was an escape from Harold, and I could drift off into another world while playing with cars or just sitting on my bed staring out the window.

Having your own space doesn't mean having your own bed. In apartment one, my brother was in a crib and I was in a bed. Apartment two came just as he was now too big for his crib. Being that he was the youngest, he got the mattress on the floor, and I got the box spring. Sleeping on a box spring is impossible. I opted for the next best thing—bags of dirty clothes that were piled in the closet. It might sound gross, but it was better than the box spring. It was soft and kept me warm. I am certain I am not the only poor kid that used bags of clothes for a bed.

Over the next few years, life's routines set in on Fitzhugh Street. I was attending a brand-new school that I could walk to. My little brother was beginning to walk and move around and despite the constant abuse from Harold, life was our own version of normal. Poor people live with other poor people so there is a sort of built-in insulation to really feel the total despair that is apparent in any poor community.

Looking back, it was far from a normal life, but it was the life I had and, at that moment, as a child, I had no clue how bad it really was. It's funny, but in some way, God shields a child from recognizing just how

bad their lives can be. This can be proven by speaking
with anyone in law enforcement who has taken a child
from their parents. No matter how bad the environment,
no matter how brutal the living conditions are, almost
always the child cries out for their parents rather than
those who are there to protect them.

The interesting thing about that neighborhood was that over time the area became more diverse. There was a huge cross-section of ethnic and economic backgrounds as homes were being sold off and converted back to single-family homes. The area was up and coming, changing from the third ward to what is now known as "Corn Hill." The third ward was a neighborhood that had always had a mix of races, and hovered between poor and lower working middle class. It was and is bordered by downtown Rochester, and a very rough part of town including one group of streets known to this day as "Fight Square." As a skinny white kid, I never ventured near Fight Square, but I had my share of scuffles anyway.

Because the neighborhood was ethnically mixed, it was not uncommon to find myself fighting with kids who didn't look like me. It was strange that while we were all poor, the neighborhood was primarily African American and as a white kid, you either learned to run or fight when walking down some of the streets. As the area transitioned to the yuppy/hippie type residents and became "Corn Hill," it became a nucleus of urban gentrification. Homes were being renovated and a new sense of community was forming that had a lot more shine than the blite of the past. Despite living in a roach-infested apartment building, it seemed as if the world around us was changing for the better.

At ten years old, there was so much for a kid to do in that neighborhood. Its proximity to downtown and midtown plaza (the nation's first indoor mall) offered many indoor spaces to hang around. There were old buildings to play in (they call that trespassing today), streets and alleyways offered endless passages to ride our bikes around—the list could go on and on. We would ride the neighborhood on our bikes playing cops and robbers. We would climb trees, explore empty buildings and play ding dong ditch. It was an urban playground if there ever was one. Outside of my house of terror, the world around me presented all the typical activities for kids to partake in. Inside, the beatings would continue, the tears, the yelling, the poverty, and despair. Yet, when I was outside, I was just a normal kid and it felt great.

The building we lived in on Fitzhugh Street also had a tragedy of its own outside our apartment. I saw my first dead person (other than my grandfather in the funeral home) while living there. There was a young lady who lived in apartment eleven, around back, near the driveway. She was pretty, I noticed that as a young boy would—super pretty even. It was summertime and she would sit outside and listen to a radio in the shape of a bright yellow smiling face. She would sit in the sun, and I would just stare at her from afar—to me she was like a goddess. One day a neighbor came running to the front of the building saying that she had hung herself. I didn't really know what that meant, but my mother and another neighbor went running to her apartment and I followed. I walked in right behind my mother before she noticed me, and I saw her hanging from a pipe in the living room area. She seemed to be asleep. It wasn't gory, and despite being ten, it didn't scare me. She just seemed to be sleeping, albeit while hanging from something around her neck. When someone finally saw me staring, I was pushed out and the door was closed. The police came, as did an ambulance and firemen and eventually, she was brought out covered in a blanket and put into the back of a blue truck. She was gone and that was that.

When I was older and learned why some people commit suicide, I wondered what happened that was so bad that such a pretty woman decided to end her life. Hearing the word suicide when neighbors spoke of what happened would also take a great emotional toll on me from that day forward, because I could connect this death with all the times my mother would yell at Harold saying she was going to commit suicide. It now had a meaning which made the threat more powerful than ever before.

Over the years, some of my mother's siblings moved to the apartment building on Fitzhugh street. My aunt Edna moved into apartment four, just upstairs, she had six kids, and like my mother, married a guy that had no drive, no job, and no promise in his future. My uncle Bill would move into apartment nine with his wife and daughter when they moved back from Missouri. Bill was a Vietnam War vet and his combat action haunted him for years. Bill worked, but at low paying jobs and somehow that landed him right with us in an apartment on S. Fitzhugh St. It is ironic that my two aunts also married men with issues of violence and drinking or marijuana addictions, and my uncle Bill, the RIT student who joined the ROTC to honor his father and serve our country, all grew up to live challenged lives. No matter how or why, having more family living there meant one thing—my grandmother would be around more. When she showed up at our building, her car was usually loaded with groceries for everyone. She would always slip a few butterscotch candies into my hand and press a finger against her lip as if to say, "Shh it's a secret."

> *My grandmother always had Brach's Butterscotch candy in her purse and always made sure she gave me a few pieces—it was our connection—and to this day I find myself occasionally buying some and I am immediately reminded of days long since passed.*

The highpoint of Fitzhugh Street for me was when I was finally old enough to get a job as a paperboy. Gannett newspapers was close by, and I went in and applied for a job the day I got my student working papers. Soon after, I had a morning paper route that included most of the streets in my neighborhood. I delivered papers throughout the neighborhood and collected the weekly charge from customers. I earned a few cents per paper, but more importantly, was the fact that I earned tips from customers. I was so proud of my job and the responsibility that came with such a prestigious job at a young age. Most of the money I made my mother would take, always with an excuse of needing bus fare or something else. The reality is she usually gave it to Harold. I was smart and always hid a little bit aside and I would use it to buy some candy or snacks from the corner store. Harold would often search my room or demand I give him money when he thought I had some, and if I didn't give it to him he would tell me I would have to quit the job. There was almost a competition between my mother and Harold on who would take the money from me first. One with a sad story and the other with intimidation. Either way, that paper route was the start of my working career. Sadly, I would eventually lose the job because my collection envelope would be short frequently and my tip money couldn't make up the difference. After many weeks of this issue, the area manager said I could no longer have a paper route. Harold's need for alcohol dominated our lives and, in this instance, cost me my first job.

HUNGER

CHAPTER 6

Hunger is ever-present when you are poor. I can't say that I ever felt "Starvation" but I no doubt felt actual hunger and the fear of hunger. Once a month, we would wait with near-empty stomachs for the mailman to arrive. My brother and I, and other kids in our building would watch for him to round the corner and then run to our apartments to tell our mothers that the mailman was close. He would be welcomed by a small group of usually women and children waiting for him to drop the tan envelopes into our mail slots. That envelope signaled the start of a busy day. We would receive the food stamp voucher in the mail, go to the nearby bank to redeem it for what can best be described as monopoly money that could only be used for food. We would then walk to the grocery store downtown where my mother would spend every penny of it.

After shopping, our walk home would include a walk across the court street bridge (the same bridge my mother threatened to jump off on a regular basis) with food in tow—sometimes in a "borrowed" shopping cart, but mostly carried by hand.

I can remember the joy at the introduction of plastic shopping bags that replaced the old paper ones. We could carry more, and we could also use them as liners for our shoes in the wintertime to keep our feet dry.

The diet of the poor is interesting and has shaped what I eat today.

Typical food stamp shopping list:
- The cheapest ground beef you can buy.
- Boxed bacon bits and pieces; if you don't know what it is, look it up. It's basically the bacon scraps. I won't touch fatty bacon today—no shot.
- Chicken thighs and drumsticks; to this day I won't eat chicken that is still on the bone or dark.
- Powdered milk; why is it silver? It smells and tastes awful.
- Puffed Rice or corn flakes—always the generic brand.
- Bread and eggs—only one loaf and one dozen for the month.
- Fish sticks.

YOU FAILED ME

- Pot pies; frozen.
- Salisbury steak and veal parm frozen family meals.
- Canned soup, creamed corn, peas, and of course, pork & beans for Harold—only for Harold.

We never had fresh fruit or vegetables unless our grandmother brought something from her garden. Even then, Harold was quick to claim the tomatoes for himself, as well as anything else he felt he wanted. Sometimes we would have cheese, but that was usually when the Government cheese program came to town. This program was very helpful in fighting the war on hunger. Every so often we would hear that there was a food handout. We would get a voucher, stand in line, and leave with a five-pound block of yellow cheese, a box of powdered milk, rice, and every so often, very rarely, perhaps a box of random vegetables or some canned goods.

> *If you have ever heard how good gov't cheese was, it's true—it made great grilled cheese sandwiches.*

When food ran out (usually by the 25th of the month) we had very few options because everyone on public assistance hit the same food cliff near the month's end. When this happened, we would walk to the salvation army downtown and get a food bag. This, like food pantry food, provides stomach fillers but is hardly consistent or enjoyable. While we were always grateful for whatever we could get, the food donated to food pantries was usually the items nearing expiration that families didn't want. It seems there was always an ample supply of lima beans, peas, and boxed potatoes or rice. When the Salvation Army food shelf was depleted, we would try a few local churches and receive whatever help they had left in their food pantry. Again, poor families are concentrated in small areas of a city, and they all know where to go, and therefore all depend on the same social outreach services such as churches and community centers. When all else failed, we would walk to the local grocery store (Wegmans) and my mother would walk around the store and put food in our clothes. More than once, I walked out of the supermarket with a small package of meat or other food in my coat or even my pants. I am not proud of it; I think my mother did what she had to do so we had something to eat. To this day, I have often thought that I would certainly fail a polygraph if ever asked if I had stolen anything. As a kid, I was like John Dillinger in the food aisle—and not by choice.

The theft of food blurred the lines between right and wrong for my brother and I. Once while my mother was doing her monthly shopping, my little brother and I walked to a toy store directly next to the supermarket. This was not an uncommon occurrence, and we would use this time to play with toys that were on display. My brother, who was maybe five or six years old at the time, put a small figurine in his pocket and an employee saw it. They asked where our parents were, and I told them our mother was shopping at the supermarket. In short order, my mother appeared and took us out of the toy store. My mother took us to a restroom where she proceeded to spank my brother on his bare behind so hard it knocked him down. My adult self wonders how confused he must have been to be part of stealing food on occasion with his mother and then to be punished for doing it on his own. I am not saying stealing the toy wasn't wrong, but the messages we received as children provided a blurred line of right and wrong.

EMERGENCY

CHAPTER 7

I remember when I was a child, my mother was always calling the ambulance for herself, me, or my brother, and always for the slightest of things. If someone did this today it would be classified as Munchausen Syndrome. Back then it had no label—at least not that I knew of. If we had even the slightest sniffle my mother would call an ambulance and have us taken to the emergency. Once there, part of our visit always included my mother stealing tongue depressors, gauze bandages, and band-aids. The only time I recall ever needing the hospital or an ambulance was when I broke my arm riding my bike off-ramps trying to act like the BMX stars of the day. I can tell you that we went to the emergency department so often the people there knew us practically by name. Whenever the doctor would see me and ask what was wrong, I would tell the truth, which was usually that I had a runny nose or just a small cut. Then they would ask my mother what was wrong, and you would think I was dying. A cold was pneumonia, a cut was a near amputation, and a cramp was a major internal injury in her world. Ultimately, every visit ended with us going home, usually walking home—winter or not. Other than the broken arm from my stunt days, every other E.R. visit ended with no hospitalization or further treatment.

Oddly, in any one of the multiple visits to the E.R., there could have been some sort of intervention or referral to social services. As children, we were not well kept and more than likely a cursory physical exam would have shown bruises or signs of neglect. Nothing ever happened beyond addressing the illness my mother had us there for. When it comes to my many emergency room visits and all the doctors and nurses who treated me—YOU FAILED ME.

The other facet of health care in which my mother took full advantage was dentistry. The local hospital also had a dental school, and we were regular patients. It wasn't that my mother wanted to make sure that we had all our cleanings and checkups, it went well beyond routine care. If my mother thought a tooth was loose, we would go to the dental school for an appointment because she would say she was concerned about how it looked. As new teeth grew in, we would be back at the dental school to address her concern about a tooth coming in crooked. We would have dental exams, tooth extractions, root canals, etc. based on her lies. Either way, at the dental school, the students took every advantage to practice and learn on kids like me. As a kid, having dental students probing and poking around your mouth or learning to do fillings and other work was a painful and traumatic experience. They need to learn somewhere, and I guess in our community it was the poor who became their subjects of practice. While I do my best to see my dentist regularly, it's always a struggle and usually involves a few missed appointments.

All those visits to doctors, emergency rooms, dentists, etc. had a lasting impact. To this day, I rarely go to the doctor when I am sick because I don't feel I am sick enough to justify the visit. I had appendicitis in my late twenties and waited until it almost ruptured before going to the hospital—all because I didn't want to be seen as someone who makes up illnesses. When I was thirty-five, I suddenly dropped a significant amount of weight and chalked it up to having a bad cold or flu—it wasn't until months later when I began to have trouble swallowing that I finally went to the doctor and was diagnosed with Thyroid Cancer. What is typically a relatively easy form of cancer to treat, turned into much more, spreading to related tissues and requiring multiple surgeries and radiation treatments. I can't help but wonder if the severity of it was enhanced by my reluctance to seek treatment sooner. It was my constant trips to the hospital as a child, for minor issues, that created this reluctance to seek timely care that I deal with even today.

I am not sure what the triggering events were that caused my mother to engage in full-on Munchausen by proxy syndrome, but I was the recipient of her actions. Perhaps it was her way of getting attention or her hope that people would feel sorry for her. Either way, as her children became old enough to advocate for themselves, she became the source of constant need for emergency care. My mother undoubtedly has a medical file that could fill a room—most of which, if examined, would be summarized as "no problem found."

While many people might say that the subject of health conditions is a common topic with the elderly, with my mother it goes much further. Any time I speak to her, the first few minutes of conversation are always about her ailments. She speaks with excitement when telling me about her doctors' visits or procedures that she has had or needs. Even something as minor as an eye exam is described in minute detail. Only when she completes her extensive medical review, might she ask how things are or have other conversations.

When it came to healthcare, mother—Again—YOU FAILED ME.

PAST TIME

CHAPTER 8

Harold didn't spend all his time sitting on the steps or laying on the couch drinking. If he had a few bucks in his pocket from doing odd jobs (or stealing it from me), he could be found at a local bar. Every neighborhood has at least one bar located on the boulevard of broken dreams, where the hard scrap people go to drink their reality away. That one place where the beer is cheap, the people are worn, and dreams of a better life are washed away one draft beer at a time. For me growing up, this place was known as the Past Time Tavern. I think a draft beer was fifty cents, at least it always seemed there were a few quarters sitting in front of the patrons who had bellied up to the bar. This was not a setting like you might see in an episode of Cheers, this was a dark, smoke-filled room with little conversation and plenty of blank faces sipping on a beer from a tall glass or a dark bottle.

This bar was just a short walk away from our apartment. Oddly enough, it was just past the county jail that Harold had spent more than a few odd nights sleeping off his drunkenness. Many times as I walked past that jail, I would wish Harold was in it. Harold would often stagger home from the bar at closing time or when his money ran out. Often, when Harold would spend too much time at the bar, my mother would send me there to tell Harold it was time to come home. Walking into the bar created fear for me because I would have to deal with the alcohol-infused monster I was forced to call dad. I would have to "tell" Harold that he had to come home. Harold would never leave with me, but instead, he would tell me to go back home before he beat my ass. What was certain to follow was that Harold would soon come home and an argument would start—then someone got beat. Maybe my mother, maybe me.

Other times, if my mother was feeling brave, she would take my little brother and me to the bar to get Harold to come home. Nothing like a woman walking into a bar with two kids in tow to make a scene with her drunk husband to liven things up. There would be days, usually right after our welfare check arrived, that going to the bar would become a family affair. When we would walk in, the bartender would give my brother and me a glass of Coke and a bag of chips while my mother sat with Harold and sipped a glass of ginger ale. She would try to coax his remaining money from his pockets so we would have a few dollars to pay a bill or maybe do something exciting like eat. When we would go as a group on this family outing, my brother and I would often play with the tabletop bowling game (despite having no change for it) while my mother sat next to Harold and watched him drink. She never drank, in fact, I am not sure I have ever seen her with more than a glass of soda in her hand.

The only thing worse than the threat of a beating by venturing into the Past Time was my near miss of being molested by one of the other patrons. I was around ten or eleven years old when I was sent once again to retrieve Harold and help him get home. It was late in the evening and Harold was not yet ready to leave. There was a man at the bar who was known for making pictures out of colored stir sticks used for mixed drinks. I knew of this man as he would engage with my little brother and me from time to time at the bar. One time he came in and had two small, felt-covered bear-shaped banks half full of pennies for us. I guess you could assume he was either overly friendly because he felt sorry for us, or he was grooming a relationship for something else. Either way, in those moments he was a friendly older guy who never appeared threatening. That all changed, on one of these all-too-common nights that I was sent to retrieve Harold. This guy suggested to Harold that I should sleepover at his house so he could show me how to make a stir stick picture for my mother. Harold agreed and I soon left the bar with this man and followed him to his nearby apartment. We barely knew this man, only interacting with him at the bar and certainly not well enough that anyone would let their child go with him.

It was a short walk to this man's apartment and when we got there, he offered me some pop and something to eat. As I had my snack, he sat with a drink of some sort and a pipe that had what I thought was awful smelling tobacco in it. (A few years later when I smelled it again, I thought back to that event and realized that it was marijuana that he was smoking.) As he smoked, he said he wanted to play a game, which was for me to guess what the smoke smelled like. He would suggest things like "does it smell like mint?" or "take a deep breath through your nose and tell me the first smell that comes to your mind." Although I was too young to realize what was going on at that time, I am certain that he was trying to give me a contact high.

After I ate my snack, he showed me some of his stir stick pictures and we spent a few minutes gluing some sticks to a piece of dark paper. He then suggested I sit on his lap so he could help me with my picture. I complied without any concern about what this might mean. Soon he said it was time for bed and that we could work on the picture more in the morning. He got undressed down to his underwear in front of me and said I should get undressed too. His apartment was small with a bed in the living room, and he said we would sleep in the bed together because the couch was not comfortable. So, there I was, facing this older man standing in his underwear asking me to get undressed and into bed with him. I don't know how, I don't know why, but

I knew at that moment something was wrong. I sensed this sleepover was about to become something horrible. I said I was sick and that I needed to go home. I told him I suddenly had a stomach ache and wanted to leave. He went to his kitchen to get me something that he said would help my stomach ache. While he was gone, I ran out the door, down the hall, out into the street, and ran all the way home.

When I got home, Harold asked what I was doing at home and what had happened. I was afraid to say what had actually happened, or what I was feeling so I told Harold that I just wanted to come home and I ran to my room. He was drunk and he followed me into my room yelling and then proceeded to beat me for leaving this guy's apartment in the dark and coming home. He was yelling at me for being rude and telling me how I could have gotten hurt coming home so late. How ironic it was that Harold beat me for coming home alone in the dark because I could have gotten hurt. After that event, anytime I went into the bar, that man wouldn't make eye contact with me. This was the guy that would always speak to my little brother and me, yet as of that day we were like strangers. Maybe I was wrong, but to this day I am sure he was going to molest me. I have no doubt. We never spoke of it again.

ELEMENTARY SCHOOL

CHAPTER 9

As far as school was concerned, I was lucky enough to be in a neighborhood that had a brand-new elementary school. I attended this school from the first grade through sixth grade. Although just blocks from my home on Fitzhugh Street, the school was like another world, a safe place away from Harold and my mother. It meant breakfast and lunch and a place of refuge from my reality at home. I have great memories of elementary school, the teachers, and my friends. I was in an accelerated learning program that gave me access to more interactive learning and involved field trips to museums and other places around our community. I had great friends at school, I had my first kiss (in fifth grade), my first fight (not much of one) and so much more.

I was a good student, winning many awards and recognitions, but I was also known as a kid from a troubled home. Because of my appearance and what was known over time about my home life, I came to be known in the school as a child to keep an eye on. I would visit the main office or nurse's office many times at the concern of my teachers. My visits would be the result of my general appearance of unkempt, occasionally noticing bruises, or perhaps a case of head lice that I either brought to my classroom or contracted and did not have treated. I would often hear my teacher speaking to others about my appearance or the condition of my clothes. The words hurt, even as a child. I think one thing teachers could be more aware of is their conversations and those who are in earshot. I was also present on more than one occasion when they would talk about my mother. How she looked, how she smelled, how she acted. These moments were not only hurtful, but were also embarrassing. I was embarrassed about my mother many times in my young life and as much as I hated her, the embarrassment became pain when negative words were spoken. The people in the school had good intentions, many who tried to help—but often they were limited by their roles or the laws in place in the early seventies.

Often, when bruises were noticed, a meeting would be requested with my mother. I would have to take home a sealed envelope from the office, knowing full well what was inside. My mother would get mad and blame me for causing problems at school. She would accuse me of intentionally showing the teachers my bruises for attention. Many times, those meetings also resulted in my mother getting a letter from child protective services that meant we would have to go to the welfare office to meet with a caseworker.

Getting a letter in the mail from social services was worse than getting a bad report card. I would come home from school, unaware of the arrival of such a letter, and find myself being interrogated by Harold as to what I said at school, or if I said something bad about him or my mother. The interrogation was usually standing in front of Harold as he sat, and was accompanied by a slap to my head, perhaps to jog my memory, and being called plenty of names such as ungrateful, worthless, a piece of shit, a little bastard, and even worse—lots worse. Then I would be sent to my room for the night. On those days, there would be no dinner and I would have to ask to come out to use the bathroom.

My mother would always blame me for starting the problems at home, and tell me how I needed to stop making Harold mad and that I needed to be a better kid. Let's be clear—I was a good kid, never in trouble, incredibly quiet at home (from fear), I had high grades in school, and was in an accelerated learning program. Apparently, despite getting my ass kicked at home, the letters and meetings at social services were my fault. Shame on me for not doing a better job of hiding the bruises and for not taking better care of myself. To further enhance the fear of these events, Harold would tell me that if I was taken away from them that I would end up in foster care and never see anyone again. No matter how bad things are, for a kid, foster care sounds like a scary thing.

When we did have to go to the welfare office, it meant I would be questioned about my treatment at home, about my bruises, and why I thought I was there—all in front of my mother. Now I am no rocket scientist but how could anyone think I would tell the truth about what was happening at home, or at the hands of my parents while my mother sat right next to me. When questioned about how I was treated or how I got the bruises, I would lie and say the bruises happened from me wrestling with a friend, falling off my bike, or any number of other stories. I would say anything other than the truth—that my life was hell, that my stepfather was a monster, and that I needed to be rescued. I was in fear of what would happen at home or elsewhere if I told the truth—so I lied. Sadly, the social workers accepted my lies. I don't know if they were overworked, they didn't care, or perhaps I was just so good at storytelling (I doubt it) that they really believed there was nothing to be concerned about. You too would most likely lie, not to protect your abuser, but to protect yourself against the unknown and the known alike.

As a child you have no voice, no say in what happens to you. Your safety rests solely in the hands of others. When there is a concern, it takes dedication to find the truth—a truth that is often surrounded by a story made up of fear. For the social workers, their job was done when the interview ended, and they could check the box

*and move on. I don't blame them but looking back I sure
don't understand their actions either.*

The one and only time I was removed from my mother's home while in grammar school, was the time Harold slipped up while beating me. I must have done something terrible like not finishing my dinner or not coming fast enough when called. Either way, Harold beat me, not any worse than other times, but this time his belt connected with my neck and ear rather than my back. When it did, it left an obvious bruise.

The next day my mom wrote a note to the office saying I fell out of bed, had a bruise on my neck, and to let her know if I was having any pain. I took the note to school and instantly found myself in an office with the nurse, another school person, and eventually a police officer. I was questioned about the bruise and this time I told the truth. I told them all exactly what happened. I think it was seeing a police officer that gave me a sense of safety. Either way, the truth was out and somehow it led to me spending a few weeks with my grandmother. During that time away from my mother, there were meetings with social workers and with the school, but ultimately, I would end up back at home with my mother and Harold. Nothing changed—life went on, and this one time when I had the courage to speak up—the system FAILED ME.

"CALIFORNIA HERE I COME"

CHAPTER 10

The school I attended was part of a new program in which children who were deemed to be accelerated learners from throughout the city would be bussed to my school to participate in this new learning program. Unlike neighborhood schools in which everyone generally lives in similar socio-economic conditions, this program meant there would be kids of all economic classes melting into one student body. This program was wildly popular and was the genesis of the modern-day programs known as schools of choice or urban-suburban transfer.

Being that I walked to school, there was little chance of my school friends who lived in other areas ever knowing how poor I was or where I lived. This all changed one day in fifth grade when a teacher announced that a group of us had been selected to go on a field trip to a nearby landmark known as the Campbell Whittlesey House, which was a short walk from the school. This landmark happened to be on the same street I lived on and would take us right past our apartment building. Somehow, my mother volunteered to be a chaperone for this mini field trip and when the day came, just as I feared, we walked right past our apartment building. As we passed the front of our house, Harold, the drunk, was sitting on the front steps and said something to my mother about who knows what. A friend asked me who that was and before I could speak my mother said, "That's John's dad." In an instant, my friends knew where I lived and witnessed the mess of a man sitting on the steps. I was embarrassed and ashamed, because at that moment, my reality had been exposed.

This moment started a story for me that grew legs and took me into an altered reality. I created a story about having a dad who lived in California. I explained that I lived there in the summertime when his new wife would allow me to. I also said that my mother and Harold owned the run-down building that we lived in and decided to live there so that I wouldn't become spoiled by living somewhere nice. It sounds silly now, but at that moment, at ten years old, it made perfect sense. By the way, California was chosen as a place for my dad to live in my story because of a show on TV known as the Muppets and a song that Kermit and Mrs. Piggy would sing, "California Here I Come."

YOU FAILED ME

That field trip wouldn't be the only time that my home life crushed my spirit at school. I vividly recall a field trip to the local amusement park. Back then parents would often volunteer to drive students on local field trips. Again, my mother volunteered to chaperone and drive some of the kids. It was a moment in my childhood when we actually had a car—although not much of one. The day the trip was to take place, all the parents who were driving showed up and parked in front of the school. I was mortified, humiliated, and hurt, when we all walked outside and saw five cars lined up—four perfectly normal ones and then ours.

We had an old station wagon at the time. The car was rusted, loud and I remember it missing hubcaps. As the kids were assigned to cars to ride in, there was a discussion and before I knew it, the kids in our car were instructed to get out by one of the teachers. We then stood on the sidewalk as the adults spoke nearby. The other cars were loaded with kids and ready to go, but everyone just waited while this impromptu meeting took place. Eventually, a teacher pulled up and told us to get into her car. My mother did not come, she drove away in our station wagon, and the next time I saw her was at home. When I got home Harold told me that I couldn't go on any more field trips because the teachers didn't think my mom was good enough to drive kids. The truth was that the car was such a pile of scrap that I believe they were concerned for the students' safety. I did go on future field trips despite Harold's telling me otherwise. Harold's words, like his hands, were designed to cause instant hurt but no lasting injury.

One of the most humiliating events of my childhood happened while in grammar school, fifth grade to be exact. I had spent the weekend at a school friend's house. On Sunday, his parents drove me home. I dreaded getting dropped off in front of my apartment building, so I had them stop a few doors down. As I got out and said goodbye, my mother saw me getting out and came to the sidewalk waving her hands towards us. She thanked my friend's mother for allowing me to spend the weekend with them and then suggested that the next weekend they let my friend spend the weekend at our house. I was consumed by fear that next week. I was so afraid that my friend, who lived in a nice house with nice things and nice parents was going to come to my house and not just see it but spend the weekend there! Remember, our house was filthy. Not cluttered, not messy, filthy—I am talking no toilet seat, dirty dishes everywhere, garbage covering the floor filthy. Worse yet, our house held a monster. And when the monster drank, he was mean.

Soon enough the weekend came for my friend to sleepover. He walked home from school with me, and I did my best to make sure we stayed outside and played as long as possible. There was nothing I could do to prevent him from coming inside as day turned to night, and eventually, we were called to go in and eat supper. We walked in and I can recall his eyes growing wide. It was awful. We went to my room and sat on my makeshift bed. I didn't have a TV or much of anything in this room, but it was away from the mess of the rest of the apartment. When dinner was ready, my mother brought it into my bedroom and we ate on my bed. I convinced him to stay in my room and play until it was time for bed. At some point, he needed to use the bathroom and when he came back he was crying and saying that he wanted to go home. Crying to me and crying to my mother to please call his mom. He wanted to leave. My mother borrowed the neighbors' phone and called his parents. Not long after, my friend's mom and dad came to pick him up—we were waiting outside. It was late in the evening and it was cool outside, but my friend did not want to go back inside and made an excuse that he had to watch for his mom's car. When his parents arrived, he ran to the car and got in, not even saying goodbye. There were just a few words through the car window between the adults and they were off. My friend never spoke to me again and avoided me at every chance in school. The result of that was not just the loss of a friend, at ten years old friends come and go, but also the aftermath of it including other kids hearing about how I lived. Fortunately, summer break was fast approaching, and I didn't have to live that humiliation much longer.

SNAKE BITE

CHAPTER 11

Beginning around the age of ten when Harold would beat me, I would often run away. I ran away so many times that Harold nailed my bedroom window shut. I also earned a latch on my bedroom door that would be used to keep me in when I was punished. Oddly, that same latch would protect me because as long as the door was closed I wouldn't be the object of his abuse. Sadly, I could still hear him and my mother arguing and eventually, my mother being hit and crying. This room was like a dungeon that I could not escape.

My grandmother was my savior many times during this period of my childhood. I was old enough to know her number and there was a phone booth just down the street.

That phone booth is still there today. If I am in the area I will drive by and when I do, I can almost see

the young boy standing there calling his grandmother
for help.

Back then a call was a dime and I always had one hidden. It was something my grandmother taught me and would tell me to call her if I ever needed her. When I would call her for help, she would always come to pick me up. I would hide in nearby bushes and wait for her to arrive. My grandmother never encouraged me to run away, but she did come to my rescue when things got bad. It was our plan and she never failed me. When my protector arrived, I would get in her car, lay my head in her lap and cry and she would promise me it would be okay. As we drove away, she would rest her hand on my head and tell me how bad Harold was and she would always say that someday he would die the death of a snake. He was a snake, and he would bite me often, and it left a poison in my heart towards him.

Soon after arriving at my grandmother's house, she would call my mom and tell her where I was. A few days would go by and then grandma would have to take me back to my mother's. When I returned home, I was often met with silence from my mother and Harold and usually, I would be grounded for a few days and sent to my bedroom. This cycle repeated itself over and over many times.

I could go on and on about life on Fitzhugh Street. It was a stable roof over my head, although not with my grandmother. It was a neighborhood filled with good people and it was where I had friends. Some of my best and worst memories are from this part of my life. I had just finished the

YOU FAILED ME

sixth grade and I was accepted into an advanced "Magnet School" program at a new middle/high school. I wanted to stay with my neighborhood friends, many of which were moving on to a nearby middle school, but I was fortunate to get this opportunity for advanced learning. I was now going into a new school, turning thirteen, and despite having a bad home life, I was excited about becoming a teenager.

As the third ward became known as Corn Hill, property values rose, and people like our family were forced out of our apartments as the buildings were sold off or refurbished for higher rents. The day eventually came when my mother told me we had to move. We needed to find a place to live and fast because the landlord had sold the building and the new owner did not accept welfare. I recall walking around different neighborhoods trying to rent apartments, but being on welfare and with no money, finding a place to live was tough. When we ultimately had to move, we had yet to find a new place to live. We ended up living with my grandmother for a short period of time while my mother continued to search for our next home. This was a strange time because now Harold was kind of the man of my grandmother's house. While we lived with her, my mother would borrow her car to take Harold to the city (aka his bar) and then pick him up later in the day—drunk. Harold would come home and lay on the couch and fall asleep. This really bothered my grandma as she always said couches are for sitting, not for sleeping.

To this day I try not to fall asleep on the couch because I can hear her voice of dissatisfaction.

The one good part about our temporary living arrangement was that Harold did not raise his voice even once. This monster became a mouse of a man—for the moment.

Living with my grandmother was not idyllic in that by now she was living in a one-bedroom apartment in a large senior living community. This apartment was just the right size for her, but certainly not big enough to hold the four of us as well. We all made the best of it by sleeping on the floor, but it was very difficult. To make matters worse, we had to be virtually invisible because if the manager found out that we were not just visitors, but actually living there, my grandmother could face eviction.

Eventually, I think my grandmother had enough of us all living there—us being Harold and my mother. The time came when my uncle showed up and told my mother that Harold had to leave. It had been decided that my mother and us kids could stay, but Harold had to go. No more drunkenness, no more smoking in her house, no more of him. Harold left, and I didn't know where he went, nor did I care. He was gone, maybe this was our new normal. Maybe my mother would see that she could live without him in our lives. Sadly, this would not be the case.

THE
MOVE

CHAPTER 12

Eventually, my mother and Harold found another apartment. This apartment was at the corner of two streets, Bronson and Jefferson, in what was and still is, one of the most violent neighborhoods in our city. The neighborhood was 99.9% minority—African American specifically and had long since been forgotten by urban planners or any social programs. The people that lived in this neighborhood lacked support services, decent housing, quality grocers, or a life without crime. It was a modern-day ghetto filled with poverty and despair. We were the only white family in the whole area, and it was strange to feel so misplaced. Certainly, we had people of all colors in our old neighborhood, but I never experienced being the only white family anywhere around. This was when I realized that classism, specifically being poor, is a color all its own. For people that are at the lowest economic class, the struggle to survive is the same regardless of skin color. Poor people suffer together and often will help each other however they can. There were many times that a neighbor would feed us, or we would share our food with children from another family in our new apartment building.

While the adults took care of each other's children as best they could, children were not as socially mature. As the only white kids in the neighborhood, my brother and I did not have the easiest go of it. Bo (little brother) spent most of his time inside. I don't recall him ever going outside in the time we lived there, other than to be walked to school by my mother. For me it was a different story—I would rather risk the neighborhood kids outside than deal with Harold inside.

As soon as we moved in, it became clear that the dynamic was different in this apartment compared to where we used to live.

1. There was a small store downstairs so Harold could literally walk downstairs, grab some beer, walk back up, lay on the couch, and drink all day.

2. The store owners would accept food stamps for anything, including beer and cigarettes. For Harold, it was like never running out of money. When we ran out of food stamps, they would lend up to $20 of credit—but you had to pay back $40. Harold did this mostly every month—for beer and smokes. It must have been paradise for him. Unfortunately, for us, it meant even less food in the house and more trips to

food pantries. The challenge for this was that when we went to churches in our new neighborhood, we were sometimes turned away because, as whites, it was presumed we did not live in the neighborhood and the support they offered was for people from "their neighborhood." This didn't happen often, but often enough that it meant more walking, more trying, and yes, sometimes a visit all the way downtown by foot to visit Wegmans to steal some food.

3. We lived on the third floor of this apartment building. My grandmother was getting old and she had a heart condition that prevented her from being able to climb the stairs that led to our apartment. To make matters worse, we had no phone so the only time we heard from her was if my mother called her to ask for something. She would then show up and honk her horn outside announcing her arrival. I would sit in her car for a while and then she was gone. She also drove a lot less in those days, so visits grew more and more infrequent. I think the combination of the violence of the neighborhood combined with her health made it tough for her to feel well enough to visit.

The worst part about our new apartment was that because of the neighborhood outside, Harold spent almost every minute inside and so did the rest of the family. This created a sort of cabin fever, in which Harold became more abusive and I spent more time trapped in a bedroom I shared with my brother. The combination of a small space, endless booze, and no ability or desire to venture outdoors made it a pressure cooker for everyone.

Now that I was a teenager, I gained a bit more independence. Perhaps because of my age, or perhaps because Harold was growing tired of us all being trapped in the house all the time. Either way, Harold decided that I could now venture out on my bike—something I stopped riding for fear of having it stolen in that neighborhood. With this freedom, I would leave home almost every weekend. I would ride my bike to visit a cousin who lived about 10 miles away right after school on Friday and return late on Sunday. He too was poor, but his home was a safer place than mine. We would hang around and explore his neighborhood on bikes, and in the evening there was always some supper on the table. My Aunt never seemed to eat very much, and I always thought it was because she wasn't hungry. Looking back, I am certain I was the reason. She was feeding an extra mouth on the weekends and I am grateful for her sacrificing for me.

I didn't always go to my cousins, despite what my mother may have thought. With no phone or way to communicate, there was no way for her to know if I was there or not. Some weekends I would ride my bike to my grandmother's, over twenty miles away. Imagine, a single-speed bike, a kid just thirteen, riding over twenty miles without his parent's knowledge. Today that would be unheard of. When I would surprise my grandma with an unannounced visit, I would usually get a lecture about how unsafe that was to do… then a big hug. At the end of the weekend, grandma would drive me back home. The funny thing was, I am not sure if my mother ever asked how grandma got me or if my grandma ever told her I spent the weekend with her. I doubt my mother cared one way or the other.

Another pivotal point about living on Jefferson Avenue was that the "Magnet" School where I was accepted was in my new neighborhood, only about ten blocks away from my home. While it was an honor to attend this school, it was also a burden because due to its proximity, it meant that I had to walk to school through some of the toughest streets in the area. To say I walked is a bit misleading, I ran—every day—ran like Jesse Owens. I had to. I was a scrawny white kid traversing crime-ridden streets in a community the police rarely patrolled. I was chased many times my first year of middle school, so much that eventually, I decided to stop running and fight back. Often my decision not to run would result in name-calling or a minor push or shove by those who would chase me. Sometimes it would turn into a fight—one that I would usually lose due to being outnumbered, but even when I lost, I won. I won because it taught me to be stronger, to be tougher, and to never give up. The courage I built up during those scuffles would eventually help me build up the courage to stand up to Harold and his abuse. Perhaps, through all those neighborhood conflicts, God was helping me build the strength needed to protect myself.

ON THE MOVE AGAIN

CHAPTER 13

Life on Jefferson Ave was hard on everyone. Other than being poor, we simply did not fit in. I don't blame the community, times were tough on everyone, and as outcasts, we became an easy target for verbal abuse, and as a young teenage kid, physical confrontations. After less than a year of living there, my mother was able to find us a new apartment that was near a cousin I was very close to. The neighborhood was mixed, and although the apartment was easily the worst place we had lived yet, it was at least in an area in which we could all move about freely without fear of confrontation because of the color of our skin. I don't think the people in the old neighborhood hated us; I think that the arrival of whites, in a predominantly black community was seen by some as the start of more urban gentrification. We weren't the threat but represented the potential for change.

Our new place to call home was on Fulton Avenue, which is in an area known for prostitution and drug dealing. The mid 1980s was a time when crack cocaine had a firm hold on many people in cities like ours. We could sit on our front porch and watch prostitutes stroll past or get into and out of cars right at our steps. On more than one occasion, someone would be passed out on our front porch from drugs. I witnessed pimps managing their girls. I watched men in flashy cars pull up and get money from guys that hung out in the shadows on street corners in what I came to know as an open-air drug market. And I saw a man beaten to within an inch of death, perhaps because he looked at the wrong person or owed a drug dealer some money. Oddly, if you kept your head down you were never really bothered. Everyone had their place and the criminals who ruled the streets didn't want to bring attention to the area by the police, so they typically left everyone alone as long as you didn't get in their way or cross them.

I want to be clear; this apartment was the worst place I had ever lived. The building had four apartments, two of which were empty and apparently condemned given the mostly boarded-up windows. We lived on the first floor, with a neighbor directly upstairs. The front door, which entered directly into our living room, had a large window on the top, well, it did, but when we moved in it was a large piece of plastic sheeting stapled to the wooden door. Harold managed to nail a piece of wood in the place of the plastic for added security. To describe the inside of this apartment is an effort that cannot be exaggerated or overstated. The living room was small, big enough for a couch, a chair, and a TV on a small table. Down the hall was a bedroom, and then an area that was perhaps intended to be a dining room. This area would become a bedroom for my little brother and me. There were no doors in this room and to get to the kitchen or bathroom from the living room you would walk directly through the center of this space. Passing through what was to be our bedroom, was the kitchen.

The kitchen was in complete disrepair, showing years of neglect by prior tenants and the slum lords that took advantage of them. The floor had vinyl tiles, many of them completely or partially missing, exposing the plywood flooring underneath. There was a sink just big enough to cover the small cabinet below it. The sink had only cold water because the hot water faucet spun but did not work. Not having hot water didn't matter much because my mother never did dishes—this is not an exaggeration—our apartments always had full sinks and counters. The dishes would pile up and if you needed a dish, you washed one. The stove was a compact stove with three burners, two of which worked by using a match to light them. The oven did not work, but it was quickly filled with pots and pans—mostly dirty unless they needed to be used. There was a cabinet on the wall over the sink and a small round table with two chairs that sat in the corner, covered with a variety of clutter.

Off the kitchen was the bathroom. There was a toilet, with no seat. This was not something new, we had another apartment that had a toilet without a seat once before. I am not sure if they are just stolen when apartments go empty or if they break and are never replaced. In at least two of our apartments, the toilets lacked seats and my mother never replaced them. The toilet did not flush because the tank had a crack running down the side of it, so the water had to remain off. When you were done using the toilet you would use water from the sink to flush it. This was not a problem because the sink had no lower pipe (no trap) so water from the sink would drop into a plastic bucket under it. I am not sure if the trap was broken or if it was removed so that water could run from the sink into a bucket to flush the toilet. The toilet was filthy and reeked of aged urine. I became very adept at trying to do my "business" at my cousins or elsewhere—anywhere was better than trying to use that toilet. There was a tub, no shower, but a bath is a bath.

I was now fourteen years old and growing quickly. Like most teenage boys, my body was developing, and so was my mind. I liked girls and wanted girls to like me. Hygiene was important and I instinctively was very aware of my appearance. I am not sure how or why, other than from seeing it in my peers at school, but I just knew I had to be as clean and neat as possible. I learned to wash my clothes in a sink or bathtub, bathe with whatever form of soap was available including laundry detergent. Shampoo was not existent, and deodorant was a treasured item that you kept hidden. I would give myself plenty of haircuts in those years but fortunately for me, long hair was in style, so I don't think my cuts looked too bad.

For Harold, he regained freedom that had been taken away by being homebound in our last apartment. His new freedom was found at the Sunset Inn, a bar just around the corner where he would go each morning and clean up outside. For that, the owner would let him hang out at the bar and pay him with beer. It didn't take long for Harold to become a fixture in the place, and I think others felt sorry for him being that he looked homeless. He would drink there all day, sometimes so much that he would end up being walked home by others. This bar, those people, helped Harold continue his climb in the rankings of evil.

As the next few years or so passed, I was able to escape Harold's abuse. I was now in high school and between school and work, I spent most of my time outside the home. I had a bike and even got a part-time job at a local McDonald's after school. Still being in the "Magnet School" meant I would have to take a city bus to school each day. This gave me the freedom to leave home early in the morning, return briefly in the afternoon just long enough to change into my brown McDonald's uniform, and then be out the door again. I was given no curfew so I would often not return until after eight or nine at night. By then Harold was drunk and usually asleep on the couch. We spoke very little, if at all, and the beatings, for me, had all but stopped. I was getting older, and

I did my best to stay away from home. When I was there, I stayed in my room, usually only to sleep.

Because my room was an open passageway from the living room to the kitchen and bathroom, Harold would often pass through, rarely saying a word. One occasion in which Harold stopped and engaged with me stands out as I think back.

It was common then as it is now, for teenagers to put up posters on their bedroom walls. For me, I didn't have the money for posters so I would collect car brochures from dealerships nearby (we lived just off car dealer row), and then I would cut pictures of cars out of the brochures and tape them to my wall in a sort of collage. One day while doing so, Harold, filled with wisdom and encouragement, suggested I pull the pictures down. He asked why I thought I was good enough to have cars like that. And reminded me that I was a little bastard that would never amount to shit. I am sure he was drunk, or on his way to being drunk, either way, I just ignored him. At some point, I went outside and when I returned later in the day, the pictures I had taped to my wall were torn down and thrown away. Again, Harold's ability to inflict pain came in verbal as well as physical abuse.

TIME TO LEAVE

CHAPTER 14

As if it were yesterday, the memory holds fresh in my mind. I was less than four months from turning sixteen. I was in the tenth grade and between school, work, and friends, I stayed busy and out of the house as much as possible. Like most kids my age, all I thought about was becoming old enough to get my learner's permit to be able to drive. Turning sixteen also meant I might be able to work more than fifteen hours per week. I could buy a car and have something of my own. Much had changed in the few years we lived on Fulton Avenue. Harold became more abusive towards my mother, and in some ways, less abusive towards me. I can only assume this was because I was seldom home when he was awake. The normality of life changed in an instant on a cold January evening—without warning, and with no time to prepare for what would happen.

The day the direction of my life changed, I had come home from work around 5:00 pm. As usual, I went directly to my bedroom with no intention of engaging with Harold or my mother. When I walked into the bedroom, the first thing I noticed was an old shoebox laying on my bed, with the contents spilled out on the sheet. This shoebox was where I kept important things including the small amount of money I had saved from my part-time job. That money was what I was able to save that my mother had not "borrowed" every week on my payday. I might have had a few hundred dollars in there at most, but on this day, it was gone. Just gone. In an instant I knew exactly what had happened, and I returned to the living room where Harold and my mother sat watching TV and I said, "Where is it? Where is my money?"—no answer. I repeated, "Where is my money?" They just sat there for a moment, neither saying a word, my mother just looking at me. I said, "I want my money back now."—to which my mother said she had no idea what I was talking about.

Now let's be clear, I had a brother who was just ten years old and then Harold and my mother. One of the adults took my money.

"I want my money or I'm calling the police," I said. In an instant, Harold came up from the couch and pushed me back against the wall. "You ain't doing shit," he said. "Who do you think you are?" He had his boney forearm pressed hard against my shoulder and neck as he grabbed my collar. At that moment, I was like an animal that had been backed into a corner. At that moment, I was strong and no longer afraid of Harold. Without even a thought I shoved him away from me. Harold stumbled backward, tripped on the coffee table, and landed on the couch. My mother jumped up and started to yell, "STOP, STOP!" Harold still slumped back on the couch, told me to get the fuck out. It didn't matter because I was already halfway out the door. I had no coat, no hat, and most of all no money. I walked to my cousins who lived nearby and stayed there for a few hours. My cousin and I are barely a year apart in age and had always been close. His mom asked what had happened and I explained it to her. Her live-in boyfriend wasn't overly interested in me staying the night and suggested that I go home and speak to my parents. I walked back home late that same evening, prepared for more problems with Harold. Harold was sleeping when I arrived, and I walked to my room and lay on my bed. I always got undressed for bed but this evening, for some reason, I just laid on the bed and fell asleep. At some point in the early hours, with my brother sleeping in the same room, I was woken up with a slight shaking of my chest. It was Harold.

I recall opening my eyes and seeing Harold's face just inches from mine. He whispered in my ear, "The next time you fall asleep here, you will not wake up. I want you to get the fuck out of my house in the morning, do you understand?" I pulled back away from him while lying in my bed. He grabbed my shirt and said, "Don't fuck with me, you WILL leave my house one way or the other."

Those words, and the tone of his voice, paralyzed me. I stared at Harold for what seemed like an eternity and then shook my head, acknowledging his words. I was barely awake, and not really understanding what was happening at that instant. Harold then turned and walked out of the room and down the hall. I just laid there for a moment, my mind racing, and worried about what he would do if I fell back asleep. I eventually got out of bed, grabbed a small backpack that I used for school, and put a few clothes in it. I grabbed my coat and boots and left as quietly as I could.

It was near sunrise and the sky was that funny 4:00 am kind of gray. The moon was shining bright, and the cold air felt sharp in my lungs. I instinctively headed for my cousin's. I didn't know what I was going to do or where I would live. The thought of tomorrow wasn't even in my mind—I was in the here and now, filled with fear and terror. I cried, I swore, I was angry, and most of all, I was afraid. It was so cold out that it felt as if my tears were freezing to my cheeks as I walked through the snow. When I got to my cousins, I tapped on his window, and he opened the door and let me in. I told him what had happened and what Harold had said to me. We spoke for a while and then fell asleep. This was the first day of the rest of my life. A life that was filled with fear and more questions than answers.

NO PLACE TO CALL HOME

CHAPTER 15

The next morning brought lots of questions from my aunt about what had happened and what to do about it. She was insistent that she was going to go to my mother and set her straight. My aunt's new boyfriend was living with her, and I heard her boyfriend tell her I needed to go home. He knew instantly that I could not stay with them, and that he wanted no trouble. He was firm in his feeling that I needed to go home.

> *In later years, I would come to understand why he was so concerned about bringing attention or the authorities to his home—he was recently paroled so the last thing he wanted was the police at his house.*

As the day progressed, my aunt told me she spoke with my mother and that I had to go home. I was being told to return to a home where a monster lived, one who had inflicted over ten years of physical and psychological abuse on me. A monster who had told me that if I fell asleep in his house again, I would not wake up. I was supposed to go to that home? I was terrified and there was no chance that I was going back home. It was a Sunday and I wasn't scheduled to work until 4:00 pm at McDonald's. With nowhere else to go, I reported for work around noon. I recall this because breakfast was always served longer on Sundays, and they were just switching over from Breakfast to Lunch. I grabbed a left-over sandwich and sat in the lobby. My manager let me clock in a few hours early and I worked until 8:00 pm, the limit at the time for kids my age. When work ended I had no place to go. I needed shelter from the cold and my cousin's house was not an option. The only place I could think of was a parking garage that was under the public safety building and jail. This garage, known as the Civic Center garage, was open 24 hours a day so access was not a problem. When I lived nearby on Fitzhugh St., I would ride my bike in the lower level and knew of an additional level where judges parked during the day, and occasionally bums slept at night. With options limited, I headed there. This would be my first night of not sleeping in a house—but hardly my last. At that moment, I was officially homeless. When you are homeless your mind becomes laser-focused on the here and now. You don't have

YOU FAILED ME

time to think about tomorrow, or anything other than what is happening right at the moment.

I didn't get much sleep that first night in the parking garage. I had nothing but a small duffle bag and my winter coat. There was only one other person in that area, and when I entered, I don't recall him even acknowledging me. My bed was the ground in a corner leaning against a dirty concrete wall. The hours dragged past until a point came that I started to hear cars entering the garage. I knew then it must be morning, which for me meant it was time for school or at the very least, time to leave the garage. I didn't go to school that day, I was emotionally drained, and I wasn't sure what to do. I walked back to McDonald's even though I wasn't scheduled to work until Wednesday afternoon. I told my manager I woke up late and didn't go to school. I said I didn't want to go home and get in trouble for skipping school. I asked him if I could work some extra hours. Because of my age, I was not able to work before 4:00 pm on weekdays so starting work early was not an option. I hung around in the lobby for a while and when it became awkward, I left and went back to the parking garage. Later that day, I visited a friend and told her what happened. She promised not to tell anyone and invited me to stay for dinner. When I left her house that night, we agreed I would come back later, and she would sneak me in. That night I slept under her bed, her parents never knowing I was there. I can only imagine what her father would have thought (or done) if he caught me there.

We were just friends, but the assumption would have been very different for sure.

On that morning waking up under my friend's bed, I knew I had to leave very early. I had not showered or changed clothes in a few days, plus I had missed school the previous day. I had to go to school no matter what. It was early, still a bit dark outside, and brutally cold. This was my first day going to school as a homeless kid. Fortunately, getting to school would be easy because I had a student transit pass that was active from 6:00 am until 8:00 pm, Monday through Friday. I made my way to a bus stop and rode the bus downtown and then connected to a bus that would take me past my school.

By the time I got to school, there were only a few cars in the parking lot. I made my way inside and went directly into the locker room. I showered and pulled out the only other pair of pants and shirt I had. In my rush to leave, I didn't grab underwear, socks, or even a toothbrush. I took a shower in that empty locker room and put my dirty clothes and duffle bag in my gym locker. I made my way through the halls as life was beginning to make its presence known for another day of high school. I qualified for free school breakfast and lunch, and although I rarely ate there, on this day the packaged sausage biscuit and orange-flavored drink tasted like heaven. In an instant, I was thrust into normalcy, for a while anyhow.

As the school day progressed, I couldn't focus on anything other than what I was going to do after school, where I would live, and how I would survive. I always had a fear of being put in a group home, so asking for help wasn't an option for me. I simply couldn't focus on anything that day. I ate my free lunch, all of it, and soon the day was coming to an end. I was going to have to leave, but I had nowhere to go.

At the end of the day, I went to the locker room and grabbed my dirty pants and shirt along with my duffle bag. I had an idea that I could wash my clothes, including the socks and underwear that I was wearing, right there in the locker room showers. There was nobody around, so who would know? Being that I wasn't sure how to do it, I did something that I laugh about as I write it. I put on my dirty shirt and pants and got in the shower. I used body soap from the dispenser to lather up my clothes and then rinsed off. I can't imagine what I would have said if anyone walked in… I hung the wet clothes in my locker and got dressed in the same clothes I wore all day. Back then pants were jeans, and a shirt was a long sleeve pullover type. It was easy to wear the same stuff for a few days without anyone realizing it.

That evening I decided I was going to stay the night at the school, and I knew just the place where a janitor would never find me. During a previous school year, a friend and I discovered a door in a back hallway that led to an attic area in the school. This was an old brick building with 3 floors, and a large smokestack protruding from the roof. I made my way from the locker room in the basement to the third floor without being discovered and then down the back hallway that led to the attic door. As luck would have it, the door was still unlocked, and I slipped in. I climbed a metal ladder bolted to the wall and found myself in the attic of the school. I leaned against the wall and watched day turn to night through some glass blocks in the wall. I was warm and safe, and tomorrow was another day.

As Wednesday came to be, it was still dark outside when I awoke. I was so afraid of oversleeping that I hardly slept. I made my way down the ladder and nervously opened the door leading out of my secret space. Luckily the halls were empty, and I headed for the locker room. The plan was to change clothes and start another day. This was the plan, but I didn't consider that wet clothes, in a locker without circulation, would take a very long time to dry. The clothes were still too wet to wear so I couldn't change them. I headed upstairs to the cafeteria for the morning's free breakfast and started my day.

This day too would be filled with fear of what I was going to do. As the school day ended, I knew I had to go to work at McDonald's, which meant a bus ride back to my neighborhood. I checked my clothes, and they were still wet. I didn't need clothes for work because I had a uniform at the restaurant. I did need socks, and I needed shoes other than my combat-style winter boots. I scouted the locker room and in the gym teacher's cage, there was a lost and found box. I was lucky enough to score a pair of sneakers that were at least two sizes too big, but they would have to do. I also grabbed a pair of socks that were in a cubby. I stuffed the socks and sneakers in my bag and left the locker room.

Being that I worked near my mother's apartment, my bus pass would get me to work after school. As I walked from the bus stop to the restaurant, I wondered if my mother was going to be waiting there for me as I reported for work or if she had been there looking for me at all. When I walked in, it was a normal afternoon at work. I changed into my uniform and then assumed my place behind the grill. Cooking was always kind of fun, and technically, I was still too young to do it, but the manager often let me anyway. One benefit of working the grill was that I could eat something without being noticed. As my shift ended, I offered to empty the trash on my way out. This was strategic in that behind the counter, under the registers, were special small garbage cans in which sandwiches that timed out (I think fifteen minutes was the limit) would be put into to be thrown away. The manager would have to keep a log of how many wrapped burgers got thrown away and then they would be taken out with the trash. I took out the trash and live today to tell you that those burgers that had "expired" in the warmer were perfectly fine to eat. You may instinctively think "GROSS" but I saw it as more food in my stomach. One facet of being poor, and now homeless, is a fear of hunger. This fear is never-ending and rises above the stress of finding shelter, or any other aspect of poverty and homelessness.

It was now nearing 9:00 pm and I literally had no place to go. I could try to use my bus pass to go back to the school but even if it worked, could I get in? If not, then what? I would be on the other side of town in the cold, with no shelter. I made the choice to walk to the Civic Center garage once again. It was about 4 miles, straight up to Lake Avenue, and despite the cold of the night and snow-covered sidewalks, it was a relatively easy walk. Upon arrival, I once again found myself in that lower level parking area, doing exactly what I had done before, albeit this time there were a few more homeless people in the same space. During the night, a security car rolled by but the driver either didn't want to get out and look in this lower area, or they knew of the presence of homeless people and left them alone. Either way, I was now spending my second night, and not my last, in this space.

The next day I missed a bus downtown that would have gotten me to school on time. When you were late to school you would have to sign in at the main office and your tardiness would be tracked. I signed in and went about my day. At the end of the day, I once again checked my locker and again, my clothes were still wet. I decided to leave them out in the open and draped over a few empty locker doors. I would retrieve them the next morning—early before anyone got there. I left school, took the bus to work, and again, found myself sleeping in the same garage.

I knew I could not go on sleeping in the parking garage. I needed a better plan. I thought about going back to my mother's, but the fear of what Harold had said was overwhelming. I thought of going to my grandmother's home, but she wasn't there. How would I get there, how would I get in? I knew I needed a better plan, but what I really needed was to get my paycheck the next day. That money, which was under $50.00, would give me the ability to do something, I just didn't know what.

As payday arrived, the stress of where to sleep and how to move around was becoming overwhelming. I worked that afternoon but thankfully I was able to get my check early and cash it. At the end of my shift, I took a bus back to my school and tried to get in. All the doors were locked. With nowhere to go, I waited for a city bus and rode that same bus route until nearly 1:00 am when the driver told me the bus was ending service for the night. He never once bothered me for the hours I rode his route back and forth across town. I told him I would get off downtown and he obliged. With a bit of cash in my pocket, I went to an all-night diner and ordered something to eat. This diner was where the cabbies and other night workers would hang out. If I had a plate in front of me, I was left alone. I was never asked by anyone if I was okay or needed help. Perhaps because they didn't care, or more likely because they wouldn't know how to help me anyway. I spent the rest of that night in the diner, sitting in a booth, watching the countless people come and go.

On Saturday morning, I went to my cousins where I knew I would be allowed to spend the weekend. My aunt didn't ask a single question about where I was staying. I think that in her mind if she didn't ask, she wouldn't have to deal with the answer. I don't think I said much about not being able to go home, I was afraid my aunt would get involved, maybe call the police on my mother, and before you know it, I would find myself in foster care. I really was more afraid of becoming a product of the system than I was of my stepfather—but to me, both represented a threat.

As the weekend ended, I told a friend I was arguing with my stepdad, and he let me spend a few nights at his house. I would go there after school and then hang out until after dinner, and eventually, just spend the night. Over the next few months, that friend, Gary, snuck me in on more than one occasion and gave me a warm, safe place to stay. He was one of the very few people who knew what was going on and as far as I know, he never told anyone. I am grateful for his maturity and kindness in my time of need.

THE PRESSURE MOUNTS

CHAPTER 16

The stress of my situation quickly took a toll on every aspect of my life. I wasn't scheduled to work Monday or Tuesday afternoons, so my best bet was to link up with a friend in my neighborhood and hope to hang out with them until supper time or even beyond. If I did that, I would stay warm and fed, but then, the counter challenge was, where did I sleep? My neighborhood was at least ten miles, and two bus rides from my school. It was winter in Rochester so riding a bike was not an option, nor was trying to sneak into school late in the evening so I could sleep in the attic. If I left school any time after 5:00 pm there would be no chance of making it back inside because all the doors would be locked.

Wednesday through Sunday I worked after school, four hours per day. On those days I had to go back to my old neighborhood to work, usually until 8:00 pm, again, I couldn't get back to school in time to get in the building. Each day presented its own challenges, each day had its own barriers that I had to deal with. The worst option was sleeping in the parking garage. January and February are the coldest months for Rochester, NY and back then, any areas that offered heat became mini encampments for the homeless. It wasn't safe, but it was warm. I used this option many times over the first few months of homelessness.

Because I had a job, it meant I had a little money. I wasn't hungry anymore and I was able to buy a few more articles of clothing that first week by visiting the local charity thrift store. I also knew that if I saved as much as possible, I would be able to find an apartment to rent. Back then you could rent a rundown studio apartment in the toughest part of town for a few hundred dollars per month. Keep in mind that I was taking home less than $50.00 per week. I would leave no extra cash, but I worked at a fast-food restaurant and got free breakfast and lunch at school so I felt I could make it work. I needed to save every penny and I also needed to figure out how a kid could rent an apartment.

As the days turned into weeks, and eventually months, of being homeless, my repetitive visits to friends' houses was drawing some suspicion and even quiet disapproval from their parents. I was constantly looking for someone else to "hang out" with after school or work, and then I would do my best to suggest I spend the night. When I would have to resort to sleeping in the warmth of the parking garage it would often result in my being late or missing school altogether.

In school, and in work, I had a small circle of friends. One might think that I would tell them what was going on, but I didn't. I was filled with the fear every day that my being homeless would be discovered and I would be forced into a system that I believed was going to fail me. I needed to keep quiet and save enough money for a place to live. If I could find an apartment, everything would be just fine—so I thought.

LATE AGAIN

CHAPTER 17

Getting to school on time was not an easy thing after leaving home, and there were many days that I did not go at all. At least once a week I would be late, sometimes very late. Depending on where I slept the night before would determine how I was getting to school the next day. If I chose to sleep in the parking garage, I would be up late because of fear, then falling asleep and often waking up too late to get to school early enough to clean up (have I mentioned how filthy the parking garage was?) and make it to homeroom by 7:40 am. On those days I would go to school, hit the showers, change clothes, and then go to the main office to sign in. Either way, if I was late, I had to enter the main office and sign into the tardy sheet that was right outside the vice principal's door. He had a habit of watching who was late and offering words of disapproval for tardiness. I was chronically late which meant I got his attention more than most. Eventually, his "attention" turned into "detention." Now for most kids detention sucks, for me, detention meant missing work. Sometimes I took the detention, sometimes I skipped it, which just compounded the problem. Skipping detention almost always meant additional detentions or even suspension.

My attendance issues quickly got to the point where I was told that my parents needed to come in to discuss my constant issue of tardiness and absences. When this happened, I was forced to see my mother. I had not seen or heard from her since I left her home and I cautiously knocked on the door on a Saturday afternoon. I figured Harold would be at the bar or passed out so it would be safe to return to her apartment. I knocked on the door and my mother answered the door and asked why I didn't just walk in. She began to cry as she hugged me and told me how worried about me she had been. I found that odd since I hadn't heard that she contacted my school or visited my job, which was just a few blocks away from her house. I began to cry as well. I told her what Harold did and how I was afraid to come back because he basically told me to get out or he would make sure I was out. I told her of my constant fear of him and asked why she stayed with him. My mother said he was probably just drunk, and that Harold would never hurt me. Can you imagine that? This monster, who has abused me from the age of six suddenly "would never hurt me"—this tells you how delusional this woman was.

I told my mother that I needed her to talk to the school and tell them I was going to be better at being on time. I lied to her and said I had found an apartment, that I was doing okay, and that I would get better at making it to school on time. I told her not to tell them I didn't live with her because they would tell social services and then she would lose some of her food stamps and benefits. She agreed to call the school and speak to them about my attendance. That Monday she called and spoke to someone who presumably bought the story because when I showed up (on time) Tuesday I attended all my classes like normal. I think I was on time (or close) every day that week.

Within about seven or eight weeks of being tossed from my home, I had saved up enough money to find an apartment. I picked up a local paper and scanned the ads. At the same time, a friend that I worked with at McDonald's said he was thinking of getting his own place. He was eighteen— that was a good thing since I was still just shy of sixteen years old. We pooled some cash and found an apartment at 769 Lake Avenue. The rent was $380.00 per month for a run-down two-bedroom apartment. We had no furniture, but it didn't take long to find an old couch and a few misc. pieces of furniture on the side of the road. Now you may say you don't just find furniture on the side of the road, but in poor neighborhoods, the first of the month is eviction day and often furniture is left behind as people move from one place to another. One person's misfortune of eviction quickly turns into another person's good fortune.

Finally, I had a place to live! This was my place, a place away from Harold. I was just days from my sixteenth birthday when the problem of shelter was solved. I was a teenager—living on his own. No structure, no parents, no framework on how to live, and how to fulfill commitments. My age also meant I was too young to truly manage living on my own, without parental oversight to make sure I made the right choices. On top of that, my roommate was eighteen, out of high school, and newly living on his own. This combination turned into late nights hanging out with friends (usually girls) at the apartment, which turned into late morning wakeups, leading to being late or missing school altogether. I quickly began to spiral in school, and I went from decent (not great) grades to failing grades. I began to alienate my friends at school because my life after school was to go to work, then home to hang out with my roommate and his older friends. I own my failures during this period. Perhaps if circumstances were different leading up to this point it would not have been so bad, but the challenges I was already having since becoming homeless put me in a downward spiral that was only amplified by the fact that I was a teenager with his own place, and without parental supervision or influence.

As quickly as I had my own apartment, it seemed to come to an end. Apparently, some of our gatherings at the apartment didn't go unnoticed by the other tenants and within just a few months of moving in we found an eviction notice on our apartment door. Back then, the landlords had a much easier time evicting someone than they do today.

Within a few weeks of being told we had to leave, we were out. Being that we hadn't found another place, Bill (my roommate) moved back home with his parents, and I went back to doing exactly what I was doing before. Living out of a duffle bag and a gym locker and finding shelter where I could. I had lost my half of the security deposit from the apartment due to being evicted, and I had no savings other than a few dollars in my pocket.

I had known the trauma of not having stable housing my whole life, but in every instance, it was the instability and moving from place to place, not the challenge of being totally homeless. When you are homeless, it is a whole new level of stress. Imagine waking up and not knowing where you will sleep that night. It compounds when that fear is topped by fear of sustenance, safety, and security. The pressure becomes crippling to the mind. It is a fear that consumes you. It consumed me almost to the breaking point.

> *Those who suffer from chronic homelessness have a tough time reentering society's norm. How do you find a job with no ability to present yourself properly? How does one complete a job application with no address or phone number—or today, an email address? Things we take for granted like a hot shower, a shave, a toothbrush, a haircut—these are all things the homeless lack access to, which in turn creates a hole they can't climb out of.*

I was now homeless again for another period of about six weeks. I had no savings so that meant no money for another apartment. I was now able to work a few more hours, but the manager wasn't offering any additional time on the schedule. On a few occasions, I would unlock a basement window at my school and then return in the evening and sneak in… I felt that if I could just make it to summer I would be okay.

You may be wondering about my grandmother during this period. The lady who was always my protector. I didn't see her much as she was living with my aunt and her family in the suburbs so visiting was a rare event. They had a phone, and I would call from time to time, but my grandmother was virtually bedridden and she had a constant dose of medications in her system due to her illness. My grandmother was incredibly sickly at this point in her life and her mobility was not good. I rarely saw her and when I did she was usually not alert for more than a few moments. I had wished that there was some way I could have lived with her. I would have given up everything to take care of her, but there was no way that would be possible. The woman who had dedicated so much of her life to raising and protecting me was now in need of help—help I could not give. I felt that I was letting her down, but there was nothing I could do. There was nowhere to turn for help for her. She deserved better care, she deserved more love and attention, and I could not give it to her.

EXPOSED

CHAPTER 18

Almost immediately after leaving my mother's house, my performance at school began to suffer. This was one of those pivotal events that any one of my teachers could have noticed as a sign that there was trouble in my life. I went from being a solid "average" student to being disruptive, tardy, failing to turn in assignments, and failing most classes. I am not suggesting they didn't notice my poor performance; I am sure they noticed that plenty because my performance often resulted in me going to the vice principal's office for a variety of reasons. What I mean is that they didn't take notice of my change and ask why. Maybe it was easier for them to not face the truth. Maybe it was the fear of knowing the truth and not knowing how to handle it. Maybe they were just all overworked and underappreciated and a byproduct of that was their lack of interest in digging into my issues. Either way, my slide from being a good student to being disengaged was met with little attempts for course correction by the adults in my life and plenty of detentions and reprimands—except for one teacher—the one person in my high school who took notice and acted on it. This one teacher took a very different approach with me and she helped me navigate this very difficult time in my life.

Getting to school on time was an ongoing problem, but I figured out how to time walking into school and evade the hall monitors. With the passage of time, my homeroom teacher, Mrs. Arnold stopped asking me for my "tardy" pass. I should have picked up that she might be onto me but honestly, my mind had a thousand other things racing through it. One day she kept me after homeroom and hit me right between the eyes, "What is going on with you, Mr. Love?" Her head slightly bent, looking over the half-rim glasses resting on the tip of her nose. I played dumb. "What do you mean?" I said to which she replied, in a stern yet oddly kind tone very candidly and very quietly. "Don't bullshit me, something's going on and I want to know what it is." This lady was soft-spoken and kind to everyone and in that instant, she found a stern voice, albeit quiet, and knocked me off my feet with her words. She then followed that with an invitation, which was more of a direction, to plan on seeing her at the end of the day for a heart-to-heart. Never has a school day passed so quickly.

Like many other snapshots of time, that one teacher engaging with me on that afternoon was a pivotal moment in my life. I walked into her classroom at the end of the day, and she told me that we were going to take a ride. She was also a realtor and she had to look at a home that she might be selling. During that ride, she asked me again what was going on in my life. What happened to the kid that did so well in school? Was it drugs, was it booze? I can only surmise that God stepped into my mind and at that moment, helped me be honest with her. "I'm homeless," I said. She didn't really react with a great deal of emotion, but she began to ask me questions about how it happened and what my mother was doing about it. That's when I told her that what I meant was, I was homeless, meaning me. As quick as I said it, she pulled her car over. We were maybe a few miles from school. The questions came hard and fast; "What do you mean? Did you run away? Why don't you go back home? How long has this been going on?" and so on. So many questions that I felt I was giving excuses rather than answers.

As quickly as her questions started, it seemed as if they stopped. She told me she would have to talk to someone at the school about this because I couldn't just live on the streets. I told her that if she did that, and if they tried to put me in a home, I would run away. It took some convincing, but we made a deal—I would let her help me and she would keep her mouth shut. I did, and she did. Mrs. Arnold cared about me and always seemed to keep an eye on me while at school. She would bring me some leftovers from home, a few times she would drive me to Fairport to see my grandmother, and from time to time she would pay me to put fliers on doorknobs of houses that promoted her real-estate business. Mrs. Arnold also helped me begin the process of emancipation. She provided me with guidance in completing the paperwork and helped me navigate the process. My becoming emancipated would allow me to be responsible for myself, without any input or involvement from my mother.

This teacher, who chose to challenge me about my declining grades, was a kind person, and always kept her word about not exposing me. At the end of the school year, I fibbed to her and said I would be staying at my cousin's house. She bought it and we promised we would keep in touch with each other over the summer. Unfortunately, we did not. There were no cell phones and no such thing as the internet or social media. Communication in those days was only face to face, via land phone or letters. None of which happened over that summer.

For the record, the name "Mrs. Arnold" is not the teacher's real name. I have chosen to change it to protect her in the event that she is still working in education.

SUMMER

CHAPTER 19

With the arrival of summer, the stress of shelter was far less. There were nights I slept under the stars at a local park (not as romantic as it may sound), but most nights I found myself staying with my cousins or random friends. Summertime sleepovers are not uncommon with teenagers so my not having a "home" was not obvious.

Summer also meant I was working more. I found a second job at a sub shop just across the street from McDonald's. The job didn't pay much, but it was under the table which meant I was being paid in cash and working as many hours as the owner wanted. I was quickly able to save enough money to get another apartment—this time without a roommate. I had also saved enough to buy a cheap car—a car that cost me $160.00 to be exact. I had a few hundred bucks and went to the local Police impound auction. There I found a Pontiac Grand Prix that had been impounded for one reason or another. I was the winning bidder at $160.00. I then had to have a key cut and pay a tow service to tow it to my driveway. All in, I spent less than $200.00 and I had a car—my first car! I guess I didn't give much thought to the fact that I would need to wait for the state to issue a new title before I could register it and get license plates. Either way, I had a car—that meant everything to me.

I worked through the summer months and learned to budget my money. Working at two restaurants meant I didn't have to buy much food. I did have to budget for rent, utilities, laundry, necessities such as soap, toiletries, etc. I had very little money left over when all was done. The minimum wage back then was $3.35 per hour and between both jobs, I was taking home around $150.00 per week. Rent was $375.00 per month, utilities and other necessities were maybe $50.00, living expenses another $75.00, it seemed there was never much leftover to save. Here I was, sixteen years old, on my own, and making it.

As it turned out, that $160.00 car I bought was not such a great deal. Apparently, I needed to have it inspected by the DMV before they would issue a title to ensure it wasn't stolen, that cost was two hundred dollars plus it had to be towed to the DMV inspection facility and left for a few days, then towed back. I saved the two hundred dollars, but it took a while. Paying for a tow truck was expensive, so I hatched a plan to drive it to the inspection station very early in the morning and then wait there until the office opened. I figured they would just believe I had it towed and the tow truck left. On the day of the inspection, I arrived about thirty minutes before the office opened. Upon the inspector's arrival, I am pretty sure he knew I drove it in because the first thing he said to me was "how does it run" as he felt the hood. Either way, he accepted the key and my paperwork. It worked!

After a few days, I called and was told that the car was ready to be picked up. They made it clear that the tow truck had to come during business hours, or they would not release the car to me. I am guessing this was because they knew I drove it there with no license plates. I paid to have it towed back home a few days later and then I anxiously waited for the title to come. While waiting for my title, my bike was my main form of transportation. It got me anywhere I needed to go and cost nothing. Eventually, the title came, and I was able to get the vehicle registered. Registration required insurance which meant more money. I found an insurance company that happened to write a seasonal policy, like for sports cars, and for under a hundred dollars I got a three-month policy with basic required coverages. I got the car registered and I was finally on the road.

With a car, I had mobility. With an apartment, I had shelter. Life was taking shape. Fall soon arrived and school was starting again, I was entering the eleventh grade and I felt my life was back on track. Despite having a car, I could not drive it to school, only seniors or students on honor roll got parking passes, and there was no on-street parking near the school. Often I would drive my car and park many blocks away from school rather than take a bus. I enjoyed the sense of freedom this gave me and having a car made it much easier to get to school on time.

With school back in session, it meant that I was once again restricted to how many hours I could work at McDonald's. I was still working at the sub shop, but the owners now had me on payroll and so again, even at 16, I was limited now to just 20 hours per week. You can do the math, but with two jobs, 40 hours per week at $3.35 per hour isn't much—$134.00 gross pay to be exact. My living expenses were around $500 per month without fuel or car insurance etc. As quickly as I had a car, it seemed my three-month insurance policy had expired, and the plates came off. Suddenly I was back to riding a bike or taking a bus to school. It also meant I was back to being late for school far too often which led me straight back to the vice principal's office.

YOU HAVE A CHOICE

CHAPTER 20

My history of attendance and tardiness came back to haunt me in my junior year. About halfway through the school year, I was summoned to see the Vice-Principal. Upon entering his office, he proceeded to inform me that I had been tardy a certain number of times, that my grades were all failing, and that I had too many unexcused absences from school. He stated I was in control of these things and clearly, I did not appreciate the importance of education. He continued to pontificate about school and my performance… "Not all kids can be made to understand the importance of completing school and going on to college." College? I just wanted to make it to graduation so I could work more. I hadn't begun to think about college.

With that lecture over, he then slid two pieces of paper in front of me. "This form says you are being expelled from school due to attendance and performance issues. It will prevent you from ever returning to school again." He then slides the second form in front of me. "This form says you wish to leave school by your own choice. Doing so will allow you to return to school somewhere else if you ever decide school matters enough to commit to doing well." This guy was suggesting I choose between being thrown out of school or dropping out. Not once in that conversation did he ask me why I was failing, not once did he ask if I was okay, not once did he ask me for any reasons why I had changed so much. Not once did he show any concern. I was in a school for high achievers, in an accelerated program, and had been doing well until the prior school year. Now suddenly, I am failing. Perhaps the adults in the school could have challenged me about my performance. Perhaps if they cared then I would have done better. But there is another thought—maybe my performance was causing a black eye on the program? Maybe because they were so accustomed to overachievers that they didn't know how to (or care to) deal with someone who wasn't taking full advantage of the curriculum? Whatever the reason I was either going to let him decide or I had to. I made the choice. I signed the form and a small card, both indicating my "voluntary" withdrawal from High School. With that, I turned in my student ID, my bus pass, and was then escorted to my locker to remove my belongings and walked out the side door of the school. In the end, my Vice Principal, and the school as a whole FAILED ME!

So just like that I was out of school and left to figure out what that meant for me. Leaving school meant I no longer had any way of communicating with my teacher, Mrs. Arnold. The one person who I confided in, and who tried her best to keep me engaged with school.

Leaving school created another pivotal change in my life. I knew I needed to find a way back in to complete my education, but I also knew at that moment that I could now work full-time. I could get a job that paid more.

TIME FOR WORK

CHAPTER 21

As soon as I was able to get my full-time workers permit, I picked up the help wanted ads and started looking for a better job. I noticed an ad for a car washer at a rental car facility near the airport. It was an overnight job, starting at 10:00 pm until 6:00 am, and starting pay was $3.75 per hour. The requirements were simple, applicants had to have good transportation, a clean driver's license, and the ability to work late. I had it all. Despite my car being off the road, transportation would be easy because there was a bus route that went to the airport many times per day. I showed up and applied for the job. On my application, I listed my other jobs, which I said I would be willing to leave if I was hired and left the education area blank. When the manager came out to interview me, he mentioned that I didn't put down any education information. I explained where I went to school, that I left school, and why. As luck would have it, the manager knew a teacher at the school. He said he would call his friend the teacher and get back to me. I had no phone so it was agreed that I would call him in a few days. When I did, he said he was unsure about me but was willing to give me a chance. He said he didn't know why but he felt I deserved an opportunity to work at the company. I now know why he gave me the job—God put compassion for me in his heart.

I worked as hard as I could washing cars, taking out the trash, and doing all I could to be a model employee. If you were liked, you got to drive the shuttle to and from the airport terminal, and with that came a few dollars in tips from the red-eye flyers. I did my best to be available for shuttle duty whenever possible. This was a good job, but less than a year after I started working there, the business was sold, and the overnight shift was eliminated. Since the day shifts were already full, it meant I had to find another job quickly.

With the loss of the job at the rental car facility, I was back in the job market. By now, I had my car back on the road which meant I had more mobility and could look beyond the city for work. I replied to an ad for a lot attendant job at an Oldsmobile dealership about twenty miles from where I lived. I was hired on the spot and started work right away. With the increased travel, I was using more gas than before. I wouldn't get my first paycheck for nearly two weeks. Money was so tight that I was out of money and nearly out of gas the day before my first paycheck. That night after work, I drove to a nearby park and slept in my car. The next day was payday, so after this one night, everything was going to be okay.

During my time at the Oldsmobile dealer, I befriended a person, Chuck, who worked in the detail department. He was the lead detailer, and much older than me. I shared my love of cars with him and asked if he would show me how to detail a car. This process is not as easy as it sounds and involves rubbing paint, dying carpets, and using products to make an old car look new again. Chuck agreed to show me some of his skills after hours and we became good friends. So good was our friendship that we found a small garage to rent and began to moonlight detailing cars for small used car dealers in the area. With this new skill, I also fixed up my old car and sold it for $1,300.00! Little did I know this would be the 1st car deal of my career in the car business. I took my newfound gain and convinced the used car manager to sell me a recent trade-in that I could afford. I paid cash, fixed it up, and again, sold it for a profit. I was still a lot attendant (the person that straightens rows of cars) by day and doing a few doll-ups at night.

There was a new dealer opening just up the road from where I worked. One day while on lunch I stopped in and asked if they were hiring. As it turns out, the owner was there. It was going to be a Mazda dealership and yes they were hiring. I explained that I was a detailer, and I was hired on the spot, and it paid $5.25 per hour. This was like hitting the lottery. I gave my employer a 1-week notice and soon I started my new job. The dealership was still about a month from opening, so during that time, I was doing odd jobs ranging from cleaning cars as they arrived to help lay tile in the showroom.

One day the owner asked me what my career plans were. I honestly didn't have any and said the first thing that came to mind, "I am going to be a police officer." I always wanted to be a police officer, perhaps because it was the Police that I saw as protectors as a child. The owner replied that he thought that was an honorable profession, but he also said that if I was a good employee, he would show me how the car business could be a good career as well.

RETURNING HOME

CHAPTER 22

Right about the time I turned eighteen, my lease was coming to an end. I had found another apartment to rent, but it would not be available for about two months beyond the end of my lease. I reluctantly went to my mother and asked her if I could move back home for a short time. I wasn't afraid of Harold anymore because I felt he intentionally wanted nothing to do with me. I was working full-time and had an active social life as well, so I just needed a place to put my stuff and sleep.

My mother and Harold agreed to let me return if I contributed to the rent (the rent that welfare paid). I agreed and moved my belongings to their apartment. I don't think I ever spent a single night there, but it was a place to store my things. This re-engagement with my mother also restarted the borrowing of money and now even the borrowing of my car.

The day I turned eighteen, I applied for and got approved, for a used car loan. I bought a three-year-old car that was the nicest car I had owned to that point. This car was a statement to me and others that I was successful. I was working and now had good reliable transportation.

The excitement of my new car wore off within just a week of buying it. It happened one day when I was at work starting with a phone call from my mother. She had to go to two different doctor's appointments the next morning and taking the bus wouldn't get her to both on time. She asked me if I could either take her to her appointments or let her borrow my car—just this one time. There was no way I could miss work, and despite the voice in my head saying don't do it, I let her take my car. The day came to an end, and she returned to my work to pick me up. When I walked out, I got in the driver's seat and drove her back to her apartment. It wasn't until I arrived at her house that she told me she had a small accident with the car. Apparently, a light pole jumped out in front of her in a parking lot and caused her to hit the pole with the passenger door of my car. The way she presented it made it clear that she felt it wasn't her fault. Either way, the car I had for less than one week and had forty-eight months of payments to make, was now in need of significant repair. I got no apology, no explanation other than the parking lots are too small blah blah blah. That would be the first and last time I let my mother borrow my car. It didn't stop her from

YOU FAILED ME

continuously asking, but I remained strong in my answer of NO.

Despite hoping for something different, my re-entering my mother's life for that short time proved to be more of a mistake than something good. As soon as my new apartment was ready, I moved out. I tried to stay as far away from my mother and Harold as I could. I would hear from her from time to time, but I did my best to avoid contact.

AFTER HOURS EDUCATION

CHAPTER 23

I was now working a full-time job that was paying the bills. I was "flipping" cars which put a bit more money in my pocket and the pressures of life were becoming a memory rather than a daily reality. I had a small apartment, reliable transportation, food in my stomach, and even a bit of spare cash in my pocket.

Despite my life finally being on stable ground, one part of life still seemed lacking, almost haunting. The fact that I was a high-school drop-out weighed heavy on my mind. It was embarrassing and caused me to be filled with shame. For me, it didn't matter what the reason was, it didn't matter that the system failed me, or that I was given an ultimatum. All that mattered was that I was a drop-out and I had to do something about that which didn't require me to give up my job. I applied for a GED program at a local youth services center and was accepted. I studied and took my GED test and got an almost perfect score. I did so well that I was invited back to speak to GED students who were just entering the program.

Although my GED was not the same as walking across a stage and receiving a diploma, it symbolized the completion of my education and the closure of my school years. I looked into attending the local community college, but for one reason or another I didn't qualify for financial aid, and paying for college would have come at the expense of shelter and transportation. Looking back, at that time, I felt I needed, not wanted college. I felt that having a GED was not much better than being a drop-out, but I also felt I had escaped the restrictions that being in high school had on my ability to survive. I knew I could still take the police exam and hoped that someday I would become a Police Officer.

My having a GED never stood in my way in my career, and most people who know me would be shocked to know that I never completed high school, let alone attended college. While I believe in the importance of education, and in fact, have three children who have all completed at least four years of college, I also believe that if you work hard you can come to have a comfortable life despite not having a formal education.

FATHERHOOD

CHAPTER 24

By the time I was eighteen, my life very much began to have a relative state of normalcy. During the week, I would work day and night. When the weekend arrived, I could be found hanging out at one of the various dance clubs in our city. I enjoyed dancing and over time, I developed a reputation for being one of the guys that many girls my age liked to be around.

It was in one of those clubs that I met a girl who would become the mother to my son. We were both young, and foolishly, we were not "careful" when it came to our relationship. We had only been dating for a few months when she told me that she was pregnant. I honestly didn't know how I felt about her, but I knew that if a child was to come into my world, then I had the chance to be a better father than the one I had in Harold. I did what I felt was the right thing—I asked her to marry me. Me, a kid with an entry-level job, no education, barely a roof over my head—I was going to be a good father and provider? This new reality, my reality, forced me to try to be my very best each day.

One of the toughest things I have ever had to do was to face her parents and talk to them about the coming child. I had only met her mother once before, and I had never met her father. She wanted to tell her parents that she was pregnant without me. We agreed that later that day I would go to her house to meet with her parents and talk about the situation. When I met with her parents, I promised them that I would do whatever it took to raise that child. I promised I would get a better job and provide for the baby and their daughter. Her mother just cried, and her father, with a look of disdain, challenged my promise and said, "What do either of you know about raising a kid? Just how are you going to provide for MY daughter and MY grandchild." I felt two feet tall, and I was at a loss for words. I had never felt so disregarded by a stranger in my life—and I deserved it. What did I know? What would I do? I had no answer to his challenge, but I knew beyond any doubt that I was going to do whatever it took. I knew that no matter my success in life, that one thing was for certain—I would never fail at being a father!

Shortly after learning of the coming child, I married my son's mother. She was and is a good person, from a good home. I was lucky to have met her at just the right time in my life. From that day on, I knew I had to be the best at whatever I did. When my son arrived, it was as if God had rewarded me and in doing so, it forced me to focus even more on bettering myself. I worked as hard as I could, advancing through a variety of roles at the Mazda dealership. I did everything possible to earn a little money on the side by fixing up and selling inexpensive cars, doing odd jobs, working overtime—whatever it took. Money was tight, but I needed to provide. My wife worked as well and together we started our young family. In the early days of our marriage, there would be many calls from bill collectors and many stressful days. Through all of it, my focus and drive to provide never wavered, there was no giving up, no giving in—no becoming a statistic.

There were many challenging times as a father and husband. I was forced to figure out how to be a good man, a good dad, and a good husband. I was fortunate to have married a woman whose parents were very loving and devoted to each other. Looking back, I was also fortunate to have a set of parents of my own that were the exact opposite of loving and caring. With those two opposite examples, as well as a love of 1950s TV shows, I tried to shape myself as a good "man of the house." While many people my age were taking summer vacations, going to college, playing golf, going hunting or fishing. All of my free time, all of it, was spent with my son.

My son's mother and I would spend the next eighteen years raising our son together. Although neither of us could say we were in love with one another when we learned of her pregnancy (we had only been dating a few months), we came to love each other over time. Our love was built on the foundation of parenthood and family. We are very different people, but together we provided a loving, happy home for our son and for each other. She is a key part of my success in life and I can proudly say that together we did one heck of a job raising our son.

A SECOND CHANCE

CHAPTER 25

With the birth of my son also came the inevitable re-engagement with my mother as his grandmother. Despite the complete failure of my mother to care for me, I felt that it was my duty to allow her to have a relationship with my son and more importantly, for my son to know his grandmother and have the chance to love and be loved in that relationship. I struggled with this, and I lacked the maturity to understand how to navigate it, but I did my best to reconnect with my mother. My decision was to allow her the chance to be the best grandmother she could be. To allow my mother the chance to love my son. This was an incredibly difficult decision given that it meant I would also have to see Harold. I would have to now face this man that was such a monster, and somehow trust enough that I could protect my son from him.

To her credit, my mother rose to the occasion. She was there when he was born and has been in his life for thirty-three years. My mother, without any encouragement, never missed a single school event that my son was involved in. She would be the first one in the stands rain or shine as he played sports. She sat through every play, chorus event, and took advantage of any other chance she had to be involved in his life.

My son is aware of my mother's actions towards me. He understands how I was raised, and how much pain I endured as a child. Despite the truth of my childhood, I have never openly held it against her in the presence of my son. To him, she is simply grandma. I have always respected their relationship—I am thankful he had it.

You may think that my mother's ability to be such a loving grandmother means that I forgive her or feel less anger towards her. The answer is no. This is not a movie, it is real life, and in real life, the real answer is no; I do not forgive her, nor do I feel a love for her.

I do give my mother credit for being the grandmother she was and is. I did my part to help her achieve such acclaim by involving her in my son's life, by making him available to her anytime she wanted to see him, by providing her with a reliable car from the time my son was born until now so she could always have stable transportation to see his sporting events, school functions, birthdays, and holidays or to take him on day trips. I have always provided her with money for living expenses and in recent years even bought her a new home that was closer to her other two grandchildren as they grew up in Florida. As a grandmother, she was not perfect, who is? There would be plenty of missteps along the way, but she was a good grandmother. Her treatment of me does not change that nor does her relationship with her grandchildren change what she has done to me. I isolate the two subjects in separate parts of my mind for the sake of all involved.

SAYING GOODBYE

CHAPTER 26

My son was only two years old when my grandmother passed away. She had been in the hospital for months around the time he was born, and when she was moved out of intensive care, I was finally able to introduce her to my son. In the final years of her life, she spent more time in a hospital than out, but she was able to hold my son a few times before passing away. Unfortunately, her poor health, combined with a steady dose of medications, limited her engagement with him but I am sure she felt some sort of happiness during those few precious moments. God how I wish she could have gotten to see him grow up, and even more, I wish he could have gotten to know her. She was such a loving, special lady, and I would give anything for my son to receive her love and kindness.

The call came one Sunday afternoon, my grandmother was gone. I remember my wife handing me the phone and my aunt telling me that she had passed. I sat on the stairs in my house and cried. I cried for what seemed like forever. Although I knew she was in a better place, I had officially lost the best person I had ever had in my life. I lost my protector, my hero, my everything that mattered as a child. The only adult that ever cared for me as if they were my parent.

The loss of my grandmother hit me hard. I was depressed and wanted to be left alone. Fortunately for me, I had a son who was counting on me to be a dad. I fear that had it not been for him, I could have taken a very different turn in my life. The love for my child forced me to recover from the loss of my grandmother. While I certainly mourned her passing, I couldn't escape my reality. My life had to move on, I had a child and a wife that depended on me.

I have never fully recovered from losing her and when I think of her, I often get choked up. There is a feeling I get when thinking of her that is like trying to remember a dream you had a few days ago. Many aspects are vivid, while others are foggy. I can remember her smell, and almost sense it in my nose. I remember the feel of resting my head in her lap. I recall our trips and time spent together. It is all right on the tip of my tongue, yet I can't quite describe it. The love of a person who has passed away is a love you never forget. To this day I feel as if her spirit is with me.

Upon my grandmother's passing, her children, at least the three girls, had the responsibility of dividing up her belongings. They engaged in an all-out tug of war over material things that had little if any cash value. The three girls divided up everything like scavengers, and there was nothing left for anyone else. I don't know what became of my grandmother's favorite things or if any of them even knew what they were, or what they meant to her. Did they know that she saved green stamps to buy the cuckoo clock that sat on a shelf in her living room, one that I used to wind on Sundays? Did they care that it was a tradition that she and I would set up her holiday village, complete with fake snow, every year before Christmas? Or that she would let me play with a cloth bag that held a few Scottish coins that my grandfather brought with him from his homeland. My mother ended up with a needlepoint picture of a tiger that my grandmother made while sitting outside, often at my grandfather's grave. Did she understand the history of that picture?

Because of the greed of her daughters, I have nothing that belonged to my grandmother. The only time I see anything that was hers is on the very rare occasion that I see my mother. That needlepoint that my grandmother was so proud of now hangs on my mother's wall, tar soaked from my mother's years of chain-smoking. There are a few small ivory dog figurines that once resided on my grandmother's dresser that now sit on a window ledge at my mother's, each chipped or broken because of being dropped or thrown. The day will come that my mother passes away, and before I call a junk man to clean out her home, I will make certain to take the few mementos that she still has that once belonged to my grandmother.

YOU FAILED ME

"DEATH OF A SNAKE"

CHAPTER 27

"Die the death of a snake." That term was used often by my grandmother when she would save me from Harold's abuse. It was her wish for him, and I believe that sometimes wishes do come true.

When I was in my early twenties, Harold developed leukemia. He was in his mid-fifties, and physically the illness hit him hard. It was a battle that lasted for about two years, and during those years he suffered terribly. He received treatment at local hospitals as well as Veterans clinics on both coasts. He was part of a few experimental trials that failed— and many treatments that brought much pain and little benefit. During the time Harold suffered from this illness, all I could think about was that my grandmother was looking down from Heaven, and although being a good, forgiving

Christian, she was taking comfort in his journey. This man that hurt so many people was receiving the impact of her repetitive wish for him.

On Harold's last day on earth, I spent a few moments by his side. Harold had been in the hospital receiving comfort care in his last days. In all the time he spent in the hospital, I never visited him, for me there was no reason to. One day while at work I received a call from my mother saying the doctors were taking Harold off his ventilator system. He had come to the day when he would be taking his last breath on this earth. I left work and raced to the hospital as fast as I could. It was an hour's drive that felt like I made in under half that time. On the way there, I had a range of emotions flooding through me. I cried, I was angry, I begged God to keep him alive until I could get there. What would I say to him? Would he hear me? I needed him to hear me! All I could think of was that I wanted to take his last breath. I wanted to watch him die—even help him die. I thought of putting a pillow over his face—would I get caught? If he was dying anyway, would I really get in trouble? I needed to have vengeance on this monster.

When I arrived at the hospital, I raced to his room as fast as I could. I entered the room and saw my mother at Harold's bedside. Harold seemed to be resting with nothing more than an oxygen tube in his nose and an I.V. in one arm. His eyes were closed, but it was apparent he was still alive. I asked my mother for a few moments alone with Harold to say my goodbye and she agreed.

I don't remember much about what happened next, other than getting him to squeeze my hand, then telling him he was dying. Telling him he was going to hell. Telling him he wouldn't hurt anyone again and that I was there to watch him die. I must have gotten loud because the next thing I knew was that I was being removed from the room and escorted out of the hospital by way of what appeared to be a freight elevator. The two people who walked me outside stood with me for a while, near a rear door, and away from public view. They stood there and comforted me as I melted away into my tears. I tried to explain to them what a monster that man was. I told them that there was not a more evil person than that man and that I wanted to see him die. They patted me on the back and asked me if I was okay. They told me I could not come back into the hospital for the rest of the day and that once I settled down, I should leave. I promised not to go back in and assured them I would not cause any more problems. I got in my car and drove home. Lucifer was dying—the monster was leaving my world for good. It felt as if an incredible weight had left my body. It felt as if my life had suddenly changed even though this man had not been in my life for years.

The time then came for Harold to be buried. My mother held a pauper's funeral for him at a low-budget funeral home. Most of the people there were members of my mother's family and her friends. I had no intentions of going, but my wife convinced me to go to support my little brother. I agreed and arrived just before the service was starting. I sat in a chair and listened while a minister did his best to speak of this man that he did not know. He spoke of Harold having a loving family, of Harold's accepting God in his final days (not true), and then spoke tirelessly of the afterlife and forgiveness. At the end of his sermon, he invited others to speak of Harold. My mother, never one to pass the chance for attention, stood up and spoke of how she would miss Harold. How he was a good husband and father and thanked everyone for attending. Then, without barely a pause—I KID YOU NOT—she turns to me and says—"I would like to ask my oldest son, John to come up and say a few words." It happened so quickly I didn't have time to think, but I replied, in a firm voice, "Absolutely not!" At which point my wife grabbed me by the leg and squeezed so tight she could have drawn blood. My little brother got up and said a few words and that was that. It was over.

Harold was cremated so no precession, no gathering, nothing—I was done with him—he was gone and would never hurt anyone again.

PROMISES KEPT

CHAPTER 28

The owner of that Mazda dealership, Mr. Roger Burdick, turned out to be a man of his word. He kept his eye on me and showed me a path to a successful career in the car business. When I announced to my boss that I was going to be married and was becoming a father, he spoke with Mr. Burdick and they provided me the opportunity to try my hand at selling cars. I was detailing vehicles then and answering phones in the service department when needed. I knew nothing of selling cars and wasn't sure I would be any good at it.

Mr. Burdick's company had a sales training program that lasted two weeks. The day I returned from my honeymoon, I left my new bride and went off to training in another city. That opportunity, one that was all part of one man's commitment to me when I was hired, put my life on a trajectory that dreams are made of. I spent just a few years selling cars, doing everything in my power to make the best of every opportunity. My hard work paid off almost instantly and I held the number one sales position in the dealership for twenty-three out of twenty-four months. The only month I came in second was the month my son was born. I had done so well that I was promoted many times, beginning with an opportunity as a finance manager, then sales manager, and ultimately becoming the youngest General Manager in his company at just twenty-one years old. It was a small Mitsubishi dealership with just thirteen employees, but he entrusted me to run it and I felt he got his money's worth. I worked as if I owned the store and despite it being a troubled brand, we made the best of it.

In 1994, Mr. Burdick announced that he was selling his dealerships in Rochester, NY to pursue a larger venture in his home market of Syracuse, NY. He offered me the opportunity to relocate and work at one of his other dealerships and to continue my career with his organization. The move would be over an hour and a half away from where we lived, and with a new child and a wife that was very close to her parents, I declined.

Mr. Burdick is a believer, and I feel that God put him in my path. During my time working for Mr. Burdick, he mentored me and provided me with skills that I use even today. Even now, nearly thirty years after leaving his company,

I am still guided by the principles he taught me. I am still influenced by his character and business acumen.

Because of Mr. Burdick's dedication to me, I was lucky enough to meet another believer who also owned dealerships in our market. He, like Mr. Burdick, gave me great opportunities to grow and expand my knowledge in the industry. I worked for that gentleman for seventeen years and have much to be grateful for as a result. Through those seventeen years, I learned a lot about myself, leadership, and our industry. I also accepted Jesus Christ into my life as my Lord and Savior. I learned the importance of faith and of servant leadership. I met the woman that would become my second wife. I fought and survived cancer, and I helped many people begin or advance their careers in the car industry. I have no regrets at all, and plenty to be thankful for.

CHANGE COMES AGAIN

CHAPTER 29

In 2010, at a time in my life when, by all outward appearances, all was well. I had a happy home life, and my professional career had brought me to the highest level of leadership there was in our industry. While things weren't terrible, there were troubled waters.

At home, our son had graduated from high school and left for college. My wife and I soon discovered that the fabric that held us together and occupied so much of our time was suddenly gone. With our son leaving home, it was clear that despite loving each other, we were different people who grew up too fast and became parents too young. We came to accept that we would be better off without each other as husband and wife and that it was now our time to perhaps live the lives we didn't when we were younger.

My son's mother and I decided to divorce shortly after he left for college. From the moment our reality of divorce was accepted, we have remained close friends. Although divorce came with some emotion, we both knew, and have accepted, that we were better as friends than as husband and wife. Our son has accepted this and although we are not a family unit, we remain strong in our love for our son and our respect for each other.

After advancing to the position of COO for a multi-dealer, family-owned car business, the owner's son became the new owner and informed me that my services were no longer needed. I was stunned at first, but in retrospect, we were different people heading in different directions. I hold no ill will and I have never looked back.

When thinking about my time working there, I can't help but feel grateful for all that I learned and for the opportunities the family gave me. The father was and is a great man who, even in the end, made good on his commitments to me for the job I had done.

My time there also brought the woman that would become my second wife into my life. Our relationship is one of destiny that neither of us would have thought was possible. As co-workers, we honestly didn't care much for each other. We were both strong-willed and driven to succeed. Our work relationship grew into a personal one very slowly, over time. It eventually manifested into a love for each other upon our departure from that company and many years later turned into marriage. We often laugh about how our feelings changed from professional adversaries to friends, to husband and wife. I can't imagine my world without her.

When, in 2010, I suddenly found myself without a job, I really didn't know what direction I would go. On my very first day of being unemployed, I reconnected with an acquaintance in the industry who owned a local Chevy dealership, his name is Greg, and although we never communicated much as competitors, our paths had crossed many times at corporate functions. I believe we both knew that we had similar business philosophies and leadership styles. After just a few conversations, Greg and I agreed to join forces and start a new business together. What started with lunch one day has turned into us owning twenty-three dealerships and employing over fourteen hundred people. Much of our success comes from our clear understanding of what each of us must do every day to grow our business. We never lose sight of the impact we have on our employees' lives. Our roles have grown to be more of job creators than just business owners. We each have children involved in our business with the hopes of one day making it their own, and our spouses not only provide us love and support but also help us navigate the ups and downs of our industry. While I am grateful for the success that the two of us have had together, I am even more grateful for the sense of peace that I have enjoyed while being his business partner. I am grateful for our friendship and sense of love that our two families have for each other as we build our empire. I am not sure where I would be had we not become partners, but I doubt life could have taken a better path than the one I am on right now.

YOU FAILED ME

FINAL THOUGHTS

CHAPTER 30

My life's journey has had many lasting impacts on me. Some good, some bad—but in total, they make me who I am today.

There are aspects of the time spent with my grandparents that I carry today. I still love tomato soup made with milk, and best with Ritz crackers. I watch the Lawrence Welk show—yes, in my twenties, thirties, and beyond, even to this day, I watch old Lawrence Welk shows from the 1970s. Not because I enjoy ballroom music, but because for that brief hour-long show, I am taken back to my early childhood. To the living room of my grandparents' home watching TV with them. I will often jump in my car and take a ride to nowhere—just me, and just to feel the curiosity within me build like it did when grandma would take the same type of trips. These are just a few silly things that I carry with me as a testament to their impact on me as a young child.

My childhood has brought other facets to my adult life, some funny, some sad, but all are a part of who I am. I will not eat seafood because I was forced to eat carp that Harold would catch from the same area of a river that bodies would be pulled from due to suicides related to a nearby mental hospital. I won't eat chicken that is still on a bone because it reminds me of eating the cheapest chicken my mother could buy.

Despite my good fortune in life, I am not comfortable being in fancy stores and often feel as if the smell of poverty still permeates from me and that I am looked down upon by the employees. If you have never been poor you won't understand this, but every time I walk in a store and carry something in my hand, I feel as if I am being watched by the store's employees.

I still carry a fear of being homeless despite having a home that is paid for. I often think of what would happen if I lost my house. Where would I live? Could I survive again? And when I see someone that appears to be homeless, I find myself being reminded of the challenges I faced and wonder how they build the strength to survive another day.

Most of all, I carry resentment for people who make the choice to be in relationships that bring pain and suffering to their children. It is a choice made often, mostly by women, who put their need to be needed above the needs of their children. It's a choice to walk away or engage with a person who, by all outward appearances, will do nothing to enhance one's life. It is a choice to suffer the pain of the relationship and allow your children to be harmed rather than suffer the possible pain of leaving, running far away, hiding, doing whatever it takes to protect the innocent children from your bad choices, and all that comes with them. I am not victim-blaming, I am adult-blaming. When you have children, your primary focus needs to be to only invite someone into your life who will better you—not just sleep with you. Beyond that, you must always put your children's safety above all else—even if that means leaving everything and everyone behind.

Some may say that the challenges, pain, success, and growth I have experienced is nothing short of incredible. To that I say—the power of God is incredible! I truly believe the path laid out for me is the reason for my success. I don't reference God much in this book because in the time of my life when I suffered the most, I rarely thought of God. I remember crying to God as a child when I first moved back to my mother's home—and feeling as if He didn't hear me or didn't love me. That was a child's thought. I thank God for hearing my cries for help as a child and in return giving me the strength to persevere and for putting people in my life at just the right time to help guide me to where I am now. Looking back, I can truly say that God had a plan for me and if even one event never happened, my life would not be what it is today.

I am still angry at my mother, but not in such a way that I openly share it with her. My mother led her life in a manner that brought great pain to me, but addressing it now will not change history nor will it heal the damage done. I really believe that all that pain, all the emotional and physical abuse, every bruise, every beating—it was all part of the path that brought me to be where I am. I don't think she deserves my forgiveness or to feel the wrath of my anger. She will have her time to face her maker and atone for her sins the way each of us will when we are called home.

RESOURCES

My hope is that reading this book will give you a greater sense of awareness about the children who may pass through your life.

If you suspect a child in crisis, please get involved. In urgent matters involving serious physical injury or neglect, call 911. You can ask to remain anonymous. Listen to your sixth sense and remember, it is better to be wrong than to be right and regret not doing something.

Childhelp National Child Abuse Hotline
www.childhelp.org   1-800-4-A-CHILD (1-800-422-4453)

National Domestic Violence Hotline
www.thehotline.org   1-800-799-SAFE (1-800-799-7233)

Child Welfare
www.childwelfare.gov   1-800-4-A-CHILD (1-800-422-4453)

SPECIAL THANKS

Thinking of my life journey and the influencers along the way, there are so many people I want to thank.

My son, Ian: your birth changed the course of my life when I was just nineteen years old. Ian, your mere existence means more to me than you could ever understand. I love you; I admire you; and I thank God for bringing you into my life. You have been the center of my world for over 30 years. I can't imagine where I would be if I never had the honor of being your dad. I am so proud of the man, and father you have become and look forward to seeing what the future holds for you and your growing family.

My first wife, Carol: you and your family showed me the meaning of family and helped me be a better person. We were so young when we met, and together we built a family. You were, and still are, an amazing mother and now grandmother. Although we are divorced, our friendship remains strong. Thank you for believing in me and allowing me into your life. Thank you for loving me, and for being so supportive throughout our marriage.

My second wife, Johanna: Although you arrived late in my life, it was at just the right time. You brought out my inner self in a way that I wasn't sure existed. You have challenged me to be more and you have always been by my side as our future was shaped. You brought me two amazing children who I have learned to love as my own—they will never fully understand how proud I am to be their stepdad. Thank you for every day we spend together—you are my soulmate—my person. I look forward to our future together as we navigate this crazy world.

Taylor and Owen: As my stepchildren, you have always made me feel like I was a valued part of your life. I have enjoyed seeing you grow and become fine adults. You make me proud and I am grateful to have you in my life.

Grandmother: She sacrificed all she had to be my protector. My love for her is everlasting. All these years later, I can still feel her presence around me. I can smell her perfume, I can hear her loving voice, I can sometimes feel her gentle hand on my head just like she would do to comfort me as she drove me away from the hell I faced at home. I absolutely loved this woman as my protector and my angel. I miss her as much today as the day the Lord called her home thirty-three years ago. I hope she is looking down from heaven and is proud of who I am.

Mother: A different kind of thanks—thanks for not very much. You made terrible choices throughout your life, despite having amazing role models. You had endless opportunities to escape the hell we lived in but chose to stay. Mother, it is only because of your love of my son that I communicate with you today. You are a victim of your own bad choices.

Harold (aka Lucifer): Thank you for showing me exactly the type of man and parent not to be. In just eleven years of my life, he showed me the impacts of alcoholism, physical and emotional abuse, intentional joblessness and so much more. Thank you, however, for telling me to leave and never to return when I was just fifteen years old. Showing me the door was the start to the rest of my life, one of struggle, one of greatness, and most importantly—one without you.

Little brother: One amazing thing that came from my mother's marriage to Harold is my little brother. He is about the hardest working, most caring, wonderful father and husband anyone could ever want. As children we didn't really do much together. There is a nearly a five year gap in our ages that had us at different growth stages the whole time we lived together. After I moved out, we didn't see much of each other. I wasn't welcomed in my mothers home for quite a while and my brother was forced to leave home at sixteen and move to a neighboring apartment so our paths didn't cross even when I returned to my mother's with my son.

I look up to and admire him more than he knows and I wish that life had not separated us as it did. My leaving his life was not a decision I made, it was a decision his father, my Lucifer, made for me. I regret not being closer to him and his amazing family. When I see how he interacts with his family, I am convinced that no matter how shitty your upbringing might have been, a person can still turn out to be a shining example of a family man. I am proud of him and proud to be his brother. I worry that some of the words within this writing may hurt him but they are true, and they do not reflect on him.

Mrs. Arnold (*not real name*), **High School Teacher:** Thank you for helping me navigate emancipation and doing what you could to keep me heading in the right direction. I have lost track of you, but I think of you often. It was your moments of kindness and concern that kept me on a path of survival. Your gentle interjections in my life at a most critical time allowed me to make it through one more day, many "one more" days.

Retired Police Officer Schneider: This person made a huge impact in my life during our time on Fitzhugh Street. Officer Schneider was a big guy with dark hair and a crisp uniform. He drove Lake Section car #233. I know this because he was always at our house. While other officers were dealing with my parents fighting, my brother and I would sit in his patrol car. He would tell us that we didn't have to live this way. I remember him telling me that if I was a good boy, and studied in school, someday I could have my own family and live differently. Officer Schneider was what cops should be, that is, a protector and a caring person with a heart for the people on his watch.

I met Officer Schneider one more time, just a few years ago, he was old, gray, and seemed much shorter than I recall. Our paths crossed and he remembered me and my family. He told me that all the cops knew Harold as the town drunk and that when they arrested him that they "took care of him" on the way to jail. I knew what he meant and it made me smile inside. He was not a bad cop, he was a man who understood evil and worked within the boundaries of his job. God recently called him up to heaven and I have no doubt his wings were waiting.

There are so many more people who I can think of that passed through my life at different times who made a difference in my teenage years and beyond. To my cousin and friends that gave me shelter when they could, to the people I worked for who recognized my potential and gave me opportunities, and many more. The list of those who deserve thanks is long, and surely some would be forgotten. To each person, I offer a sincere thank you.

ABOUT THE AUTHOR

John Love lives with his wife in Rochester, NY. He is a successful businessman who owns over 20 businesses, employing over 1,400 people. John took the experiences of his life as a neglected, abused child and used them to become a strong, caring, and compassionate adult. John's journey further questions the influence of Nature or Nurture as the predominant force in our growth from child to adult.

Made in the USA
Middletown, DE
26 October 2022

13579862R00106